EVERYDAY BIRDS

Everyday Birds

TONY SOPER

Illustrations by Robert Gillmor

DAVID & CHARLES
NEWTON ABBOT LONDON
NORTH POMFRET (VT) VANCOUVER

By the same author:
The New Bird Table Book
Wildlife Begins at Home
The Shell Book of Beachcombing
The Wreck of the Torrey Canyon
(with Crispin Gill and Frank Booker)
Penguins (with John Sparks)
Owls (with John Sparks)

ISBN 0 7153 7277 7
Library of Congress Catalog Card Number
76 20134

Set in 12 on 13 point Bembo
and printed in Great Britain
at the Alden Press, Oxford
for David & Charles (Publishers) Limited
Brunel House Newton Abbot Devon

Published in the United States of America
by David & Charles Inc
North Pomfret Vermont 05053 USA

Published in Canada
by Douglas David & Charles Limited
1875 Welch Street North Vancouver BC

CONTENTS

For
Timothy Jan Soper
and
Emily Mary Gillmor

LIST OF ILLUSTRATIONS

List of Illustrations

PHOTOGRAPHS

1 EVERYDAY BIRDS

Ospreys and blue-cheeked bee-eaters are all very well, bursting into the headlines with their over-heated rarity, but sparrows and starlings are just as interesting and a great deal easier to see. But if you say that to the average birdwatcher you get a very old-fashioned look. For sparrows are generally regarded as boring brown birds, and creatures like swans and pigeons are barely admitted to be birds at all. Yet the fascination of rarity is shallow. Should one sad, misguided yellow-browed warbler take a wrong turn on its journey across North America, and should the wind blow a bit harder than usual, so that in no time at all the unfortunate bird finds itself making an exhausted landfall on the wild coast of Wales or Scotland or the south-west: what welcome does it get, in this strange and unexpected land? A few days of quiet recuperation, sampling the exotic foods of this fabled shore, before settling down to endure a few months' isolation? Not at all. Before he can squeak a few tentative calls of friendship, some monstrous mammal, be-slung with cameras and staring through expensive glasses, homes in on the rarity and whoops with joy. The immigrant is hounded from bush to bush, stared at and photographed for posterity, for all the world as if there was some great significance in its arrival. The only time I ever took part in one of these jamborees it ended in the death of the bird, which in its tired and hungry state was deprived of both the things it needed: food and rest. Since then I've reckoned that the best thing to do with a rarity is to leave it alone.

Some birdwatchers have a curious attitude to birds which are easily seen and enjoyed, those which have thrown in their lot with us – robins, sparrows, starlings. They don't want to bother about them. Most especially they deprecate the birds which have enjoyed the slippery slope of domestication and reached a partnership with man. They feel that the swans, mallards and pigeons which enjoy our parks and gardens ought to be flying the Arctic wastes or haunting the seacoast of their ancestors. But that's nonsense. What a biological desert the centre of a city would be without the clapping wings, the graceful flight and seductive cooing of pigeons. How much more loneliness would there be if people couldn't feed the odd crust to a seagull or a gang of sparrows. They make a mess, it's true. But at least it's a straightforward dollop of nitrogen-rich manure, much welcomed by plants. Some of the messes we make ourselves are a great deal less wholesome, and are jettisoned quietly far out at sea, where millions of creatures die quietly without littering our doorstep. So let's take pleasure and companionship with those commensal species – the ones which flatter us by sharing our table.

There is of course a severely practical and essential relationship between birds and men. Quite apart from their value as a primary food source, they are natural controllers of agricultural 'pests', agents for the propagation and pollination of plants, and so on. But in this book we are more concerned with the simple pleasures of knowing something about the lifestyle of some of those species most likely to cross our paths. Their songs liven up the spring, and their colour and movement enrich the garden and park all through the year. They come in all shapes and sizes, and those shapes and sizes have been achieved after a long process of trial and error, so they represent supreme fitness for purpose. Beaks, for instance. A sparrow has a powerful nutcracker bill, and he is an expert at husking corn and other seeds. A robin has a delicate probing bill which seeks and destroys soft grubs and worms. Ducks' feet are for paddling, blue tits' feet are for grasping. And so on. Just by having a good look at an animal we ought to be able to say something about the way it lives, even if we've never seen it before and don't know what kind of country it inhabits.

All animals are interesting, but not all are popular. Television film-makers don't queue up for the privilege of filming 'the private life of the slug', and we don't much like spiders or mosquitoes or snakes. But generally speaking, birds are welcome, with certain reservations about 'bullies' like sparrows and starlings. So what is it about birds which makes them popular? Mammals, are, after all, superior in brain development and have a more complex relationship between parent and young. But, with some exceptions, wild mammals tend to be shy, nocturnal creatures, not easy to make friends with. And, apart from the bats, which are hardly popular anyway, they are solidly earthbound, like us. What sets birds apart, and gives them that extra attraction is the fact that they can fly. Mammals may be masters down below, but birds are lords of the sky, and that makes powerful magic for our imaginations. It is, to say the least, an enviable facility, and men have spent some thousands of years in splendid and expensive attempts to join the club.

As every aircraft designer knows, flight requires good design: a light airframe and a powerful engine. Birds pursued their own research and development programme from their earliest earthbound model, a lizard. That lizard had four legs, but walked mainly on the hind pair. The front ones were available for experiment, and they became modified into wings. The skeleton was already light and strong, the bones hollow; useful qualities, improved by some strengthening struts which held the airframe rigid. A bird's muscle represents a third of its body weight, and this power plant is conveniently located under the centre of lift – an aid to stability in flight. The engineering problems were overcome during a very long trial period. For birds, like test pilots, the penalty for failure is severe, and no new model survived long if the design was not impeccable.

The supreme engineering triumph of the bird is its feathers: purpose-built extensions of the skin, horny growths similar in origin to our own fingernails. Light but strong, amongst other things they provide lift surfaces which, powered by all that muscle, give the bird flight capability. Their surface area is large, compared with the weight involved, and their ingenious design allows for continuous maintenance and ruffle-smoothing. And when a part has come to the end of its useful life, after much wear and tear, it may be replaced without withdrawing the aircraft from service.

The power of flight gives birds the key to world travel. A tern may spend the summer nesting in the Arctic, then strike south to 'winter' in the Antarctic, incredible though that may seem to us. From its point of view it is simply making the best of both worlds. Not all birds use those feathers to propel them across the world. Flight has other values. Instant escape from enemies, airborne invasion of an area rich in caterpillars, or fast approach and capture of prey: all these things are possible with feathers. And different birds have different designs to fit them best for different purposes. A swift has narrow, swept-back wings, designed for speed and aerial fly-chasing; its take-off and landing performance is poor. A pheasant has broad, short wings, giving a powerful near-vertical take off for instant escape, although it pays for the facility by having a low endurance, needing to land again within a short distance – far enough away, though, to keep out of trouble.

Even for flightless birds, which might at first seem to make nonsense of all those years of research and development, the wings are important pieces of equipment. A penguin's flipper may seem an un-feather-like, hard, rigid structure, but it is in fact a modified wing superbly built for flying – *underwater*; the bird is a master submariner.

Wings are not only used for flying. They may be used as legs, as when a swallow struggles to take a few shaky steps on the ground. On occasion they may be used as advertisement hoardings, their colour-reflecting surfaces being held up and displayed in order to intimidate a rival or impress a partner. The wings are then playing their part in the process of avian communication.

Feathers, too, have functions beyond providing lift and flight. Soft down feathers insulate the body and keep it warm; waterproof outer contour feathers repel rain and keep it dry. In some species feathers may help to guide flying insects into the gaping maw and in others feathers may protect the face from the stings of bees and wasps. So feather maintenance looms large in a bird's daily life. Much time is devoted to bathing, oiling and preening, keeping the tools of the trade in trim and keeping the bird dry, warm and ready for instant take off. If they are badly damaged, they are replaced as part of normal growth. In the ordinary course of wear and tear they will be replaced as part of a continuous moult: a continuous, but staggered process for obvious reasons – at any given time the bird must not be at a disadvantage with too many feathers out of action. Ducks and geese do in fact follow a somewhat different plan, moulting all their flight feathers in one fell swoop, lying doggo and flightless for a few weeks after the breeding season while they grow a new suit for the migration flight. At this period they present a sorry appearance, but even this 'eclipse' plumage serves a purpose, camouflaging the birds at the time when they are most vulnerable.

Birds have a great sense of adventure, which appeals to us. They will go anywhere, do anything, and have an aptitude for taking advantage of a situation. So it's not surprising that they have learnt the benefits of living with man. Kestrels patrol the motorway verges and take over the remote ledges of high-rise flats, building nests of scrap wire from the factory yard. Pigeons court the lunchtime sandwich-eater, and robins follow the spade. One way and another, these feathered animals have an awesome ability to make a living wherever there's a living to be made. Where there's anything edible there's a bird of some sort eating it. There are specialist birds in every field – and in the air, in the desert, at sea, and so on. They come in all shapes and sizes and pursue a variety of ingenious lifestyles. And quite as interesting as any of the far-flung adventurers are the birds which live next door to us. There is a lifetime of interest and pleasure to be gained from making friends with bird neighbours. And surely being friends with birds is a moderate step towards being friends with people.

There are of course plenty of ways of influencing and persuading birds to share their lives with us. Providing food, in the shape of berry-bearing shrubs and trees, seed-producing plants, and directly from our table scraps, is the first step. Providing nesting places, whether natural ones in or on trees and hedges, or artificial ones in nestboxes, is the next. There are those who take a purist attitude and say that it is wrong to feed and shelter wild birds. But this is to perpetuate the long-standing nonsense that man is set apart from the other animals as some form of separate being, whereas in plain truth we are not; we are simply superior in brain power to the rest. Whether we like it or not, we are the dominant species, for the moment at least, and we must learn to exercise our responsibility in the community to which we belong. In everything we do we 'interfere' in the natural course of events, sometimes with disastrous results, sometimes with happy ones. We have no choice but to keep trying, with at least the intention of making life for all of us pleasanter and more interesting.

The most obvious way we can learn to understand and appreciate our place and our purpose in the grand scheme is to know something of those animals which, for one reason or another, choose to live alongside us: familiar, but in no sense contemptible. For myself, and I freely admit my ignorance, I find more and more pleasure in trying to grasp the intricacies of doorstep life. Parochial and inward-looking it may seem at first sight; but the more you think about it the more global are the implications of everything that happens around your own family circle. Everyday life is far more exciting than the glamorous artificial life of far-flung explorers and kite-flyers, and everyday birds are the most rewarding of all.

2 HEAR MY SONG ... THE ROBIN

Not the most common bird in Britain, but possibly the best known. Certainly a favourite. It's not always easy to define what makes an animal popular, but this is the classic case of a favoured species: plump and jaunty, colourful and tame, easily recognised and with a flattering predilection for human companionship; a general charm of disposition, at least towards you and me. The large, dark eyes are particularly attractive, set over a slender and delicate bill; olive-brown upper parts, bright red-orange forehead, throat and breast, with a pale grey border. The sexes look alike, though the full glory only comes with maturity – the spotty young lacking the red breast. They all behave, to our eyes, in a mild and moderate manner, hopping about with frequent flickings of the wings and tail. At the sight of a mealworm – or an intruder – the bobbing and flicking becomes more excitable, and the iron fist stiffens inside the velvet glove.

A bird of woodland edge, hedgerows, stream valleys, scrub country and, less commonly, of the dense undergrowth in woodlands, yet always happy to co-habit with man, the flowering of suburban gardens came as manna from heaven for the robin, who promptly colonised this brand-new habitat and took it for his own. Perfectly able to survive independently of man, he nevertheless sees where bread is buttered and takes full advantage of the purpose-built complex of food, shelter and protection provided by rows of potential nest-buildings and pocket-handkerchiefs of fruit and veg. If it weren't for our inexplicable fondness for cats, suburban Britain would be a robin paradise. Sparrowhawks and small boys are thin enough on the ground for them to cope. They need a patch of open country over which to forage, but dense cover in which to retreat when attacked by enemies. The last requirement for everyday robin living is a song-post from which to proclaim the news, and that, too, in the shape of a tall tree or a clothes post, is readily available.

Robins tend to perch on a branch, keeping a sharp eye on the surroundings, then when an insect shows itself there's a brief sortie to collect it, and return. In the wild, their food is mainly insects, especially beetles and flies, but they'll take spiders and earthworms freely enough, and some fruit, berries and weed seeds. So it is clear why they are such enthusiastic gardeners, always ready to join in with a spot of digging.

> Up on the ditcher's spade thou'lt hop
> for grubs and wreathing worms to search;
> Where woodmen in the forest chop,
> Thou'lt fearless on their faggots perch.
>   (John Clare, *The Autumn Robin*)

Everyone knows that robins are fond of crumbs, but mealworms are their favourite titbit, followed closely by cheese. They are enthusiastic birdtable customers, prepared to sample

Courtship feeding by male, on left

Threat display, showing off the red breast to an intruder above the displaying bird

anything that's going. Their birdtable technique is much the same as their typical twig-to-ground forays for wild food: appraisal from a safe distance, then the firm approach and grab, and removal of the food to a safe place for enjoyment. They will soon learn to come and tap on the window for a daily ration of currants or sultanas. Some individuals have even learnt to take their turn on the peanut bag, along with the tits and greenfinches.

One of the reasons for the robin's popularity is that his presence can be relied on as a familiar and sedentary resident. Unlike the summer or winter visitors, or passage migrants, he can be counted on to put in a regular daily appearance. Even the garden tits and finches, certainly the sparrows, will take a break at certain times of year, when they find more attractive feeding away from the garden, but the robin stays at home. However, there is one short period of the year when he becomes somewhat shy, and may only visit the bird table with extra diffidence: during the period of the annual post-breeding moult. In late summer, while his used plumage is being shed and before the splendid new battle-colours flower, he will shrink into the shadows and, untypically, keep himself to himself. At this time he won't even sing.

In fact, while it is true that the male birds, especially in the southern part of the British Isles, and especially those living in gardens, are stay-at-homes, the same is nothing like so true of the females. Unfortunately there are very few recoveries of ringed robins, but what evidence there is seems to suggest that, after the breeding season, many females fly south and find their way across the channel to northern France and the Biscay coast of France and Spain. They return early in the New Year. Curiously enough, at the same time as they fly away, there is a considerable reverse traffic of continental birds flying to winter in England. A separate race, these visitors are markedly paler in colour, but their main difference is in their behaviour: they are very much less confiding, and tend to make for the more traditional woodland habitats – not surprising in view of the

'Robins have a fancy for an unusual range of nest-sites' (*Eric Hosking*)

prevailing continental attitude that the robin is a tasty morsel,
suitable quarry for the hunter.

Even in the short dark days of winter, the garden robin sings.
While most birds are silent, or at best twittering feeding calls,
and at worst thousands of miles away, our robin entertains us
with full song. Apart from the short moulting break he sings
right throughout the year, for which much thanks! So it's not
surprising that we develop such a fondness for the garden
redbreast. He appears such a permanent resident that it seems
churlish to point out that your garden familiar may in fact, over
a period of years, be a whole succession of individuals following
each other as life's disasters take their toll. All robins look alike
to us, and you'll need to work very hard to learn to distinguish
individuals. When a robin dies he leaves vacant a comfortable
'freehold property', and there's precious little delay before a

new occupant arrives. Robins are not particularly long-lived. The record is currently held by an Irish bird which lasted eleven years, and other ringed birds have approached that span, but these are exceptions. The average lifespan is said to be little more than a year. So there's small doubt that 'our' robin is a string of individuals over any period of years. One thing we can be sure of: there won't be an extended period of vacancy when one dies. The garden won't stay long without its badge of flashing red.

In folklore, robins are pious birds: a dull brown bird is said to have plucked a thorn from Jesus' crown, wounding its own breast in the process, a stain which has remained ever since as a badge of honour.

And the 'pious bird with a scarlet breast' improved his reputation over the years by undertaking the task of covering the bodies of dead men in the woods. 'The robin redbreast, if he find a man or woman dead, will cover his face with moss; and some think if the body should remain unburied he will cover the whole body' (Johnson, *Cornucopia*).

When Victorian postmen sported waistcoats of ruddy hue, these welcome callers soon became known as 'robins'. The bird which was earlier associated with the crucifixion became a symbol of Christmas, as portrayed on Christmas cards delivered by 'robins'. And since Christmas is a time for warmth and fellowship amongst men, those desirable attributes were transferred by the greetings-card industry to the character of the already popular bird. On Christmas cards, ruddy-breasted robins clustered on the snowy spruce and carolled goodwill.

Real-life robins of course possess no such admirable bonhomie. With all their undoubted good points it's almost a relief to find that there is a darker side to their character. For they are thoroughly unsociable. Barely able to tolerate their own mates long enough to complete the breeding cycle, they won't tolerate another robin anywhere near them in everyday life. Once the breeding season is over, a robin moults his feathers. At this time of disadvantage, when he doesn't look good and his flying gear is well below par, he skulks quietly out of sight. But such unaccustomed reserve is shortlived. With a new coat of feathers he bursts into song, loud and clear, establishing ownership of his freehold site, ripe for development. Cock birds, and in many cases hens too, sing in autumn – a powerful voice, warbling melodious and liquid phrases, proclaiming land ownership and actively defending it against all comers. Trespassers will be prosecuted, they sing, though a desirable female will be tolerated. So in August and September open warfare breaks out in suburban gardens. The weapons are song and posture, all the panoply of aggressive display. Belting out snatches of song, the robin sways and jerks, flicking his tail and wing. With his head well up he puffs out his chest and flaunts the red flag, threatening his rival and telling him to drop dead or at the very least to push off, soon. If the intruder doesn't get the message the birds may actually come to blows, interspersed with much posturing and swaying. Territory is very precise, and a newcomer soon knows exactly where he may or may not show his face without trouble.

In all this performance the redness of the breast is crucial, releasing innate – instinctive – reactions. Indeed all the song and fury of a robin who feels his property threatened will be elicited by the introduction of a stuffed robin into the area, provided only that the red breast feathers are on display. The robin has excellent eyesight, and is perfectly capable of distinguishing between a live bird and a dead one, but the red feathers are just too much for him. It was David Lack in *The Life of the Robin*, one of the classic pioneer studies of animal behaviour, who showed that the robin's posturing and territorial display is entirely instinctive and programmed to a rigid formula, in no way allowing for intelligent modification of variation. Faced with the red breast of an intruding robin, *or a bundle of red feathers*, the incumbent must confront him, or it, with a threat display. And a wonderfully economical way of waging war it

'You dig the garden, I'll eat the worms. . .' (*Eric Hosking*)

24

is, for in the great majority of cases the challenger promptly faces about and tries his luck elsewhere, and no blood is shed.

But what is the purpose of it all? Since this posturing and fighting is so much a part of robin life it just has to be important for survival. Presumably it plays some part in ensuring that the distribution of robins is matched to the available food supply, food being the overriding factor determining the population level of any species. A bird unable to secure a breeding territory does not breed, so there is a check on population. The bird with a property is assured of a living. It must defend that property against all comers. All birds claim some kind of territory, but robins are extraordinarily pugnacious in its defence. One individual even went so far as to transfer his rage to the person of an innocent bantam cock which shared a feeding place. The red comb on top of the bantam's head suggested an intruder.

A curious defence problem arises when a robin, or any of several other garden birds for that matter, comes face to face with a mirrored surface while he is patrolling his territory. A reflecting window, the wing mirror of a car or a gleaming hub-cap will produce a violent reaction from the bird which sees its own image. Faced with what appears to be an intruding male trespassing on his property and doubtless about to take over and make advances to the ladies, he has to respond. He raises himself to his full height and puts on his most threatening display. In the ordinary way the trespasser reconsiders very quickly, flies off, and that's the end of that. But with the glass acting as a mirror, our hero finds his aggressive posture returned. He gets mad. His mirror image gets mad. He attacks and pecks the glass. This can go on for a long time and waste a great deal of energy. There's something pathetic about the sight of an unfortunate robin, or wagtail, or blackbird, perching on the bonnet of a car, displaying like crazy at his own mirror image, screaming blue murder and getting nowhere. So if you find this happening, do please make life easier for the bird by covering the mirror or whatever it is. That effectively removes the intruder and restores a little peace.

One bushe can not harbour two Robin redbreasts
(Proverb, 1583).

Once established on an estate of his own, a cock robin advertises for a mate. He may pair at any time from the middle of December, and the two birds will spend some time deciding on a nest-site, but the building work is delayed till March. This close contact between two members of such a pugnacious species is not attained without due ration of ritual. While many birds indulge in spectacular courtship displays, with much chasing and rough-and-tumble, billing and cooing, the robin's is not a flamboyant affair. But the pair will enjoy courtship feeding, where the hen behaves in juvenile fashion, trembling her wings and begging for food, expecting to be handed a choice morsel by the cock. This activity cements the bond between the couple and helps to strengthen the sex drive. In the

ordinary way birds are reluctant to risk close physical proximity even with others of their own species, and clearly this inhibition has to be overcome if any eggs are going to be fertilised. So courtship feeding obviously has much more than token value. It allows time for the two to get together in the context of an innocuous activity which does not at first sight have sexual significance.

Robins have a fancy for an unusual range of nest-sites, though mostly they go for a hedge-bank or a large hole in a wall, especially if it is well obscured with creeper or ivy. Discarded tin cans, buckets, kettles, are all pressed into service, while if they can gain access to a shed or house they will build on a shelf or in a coat pocket. A robin even started one morning to build in someone's bedroom, choosing the attractive folds and comfort of an unmade bed. (In this event the bed and room were made over to the robin till the resulting family was successfully fledged.) Once a robin has learnt to find food inside a house, it will soon discover all the various methods of entrance; if one window is shut it will try another, mapping the internal geography of the house and threading its way about the labyrinth of passages and stairs and rooms.

But wherever the nest site, it is usually in the vicinity of hedgerows or gardens. It is built single-handed by the female, a foundation of dead leaves and moss, lined with hair and maybe the odd feather. A bulky structure, but well hidden. Robins' nest are not in the least easy to find. Once built, the hen invites the cock to copulate, and again, like the earlier stages of courtship, the ritual is not a showy affair. She lowers her head, crouching in a flattened position, and the cock bird mounts and treads. This performance will take place several times during the period of egg-laying, while the nest-cup is furnished with about half-a-dozen white eggs, freckled with reddish markings. Incubation is by the hen only, and at this time the courtship feeding is more in earnest, as the cock nourishes the hen who must sit tight for the fortnight of brooding. There may be two, or even three, successive families in the same nest.

At the end of the season the adults retire for a few weeks to moult, renewing their plumage so that they can face the world in splendour again. Apart from that brief withdrawal, cock robin sings his triumphant song day in, day out.

No noise is here, or none that hinders thought.
The redbreast warbles still, but is content
With slender notes, and more than half suppressed:
Pleased with his solitude, and flitting light
From spray to spray, where'er he rests he shakes
From many a twig the pendent drops of ice,
That tinkle in the withered leaves below.
Stillness, accompanied with sounds so soft,
Charms more than silence.

(William Cowper, *The Robin in Winter*)

3 BLACKBIRD ... THE EARLY BIRD

Plump and rounded, black and beautiful, but with a touchy disposition, rattling off to cover with a high-pitched chatter at the least upset. A beautiful voice, yet a noisy bird, with a particularly tiresome chik-chik-chik in the evening when it's going to roost, or making faces at cats or owls. One of the three commonest land birds in Britain (with the house sparrow and starling); a successful species, which like the robin has come to terms with man.

In the mid-nineteenth century the blackbird was very much a woodland bird, but it has slowly and steadily become acclimatised, first to gardens, then to the urban delights of city parks and green places. In eastern Europe it still is a woodland bird, but with us it has learnt the advantages and pleasures of association. It is expanding its range, penetrating into higher northern latitudes. Already it breeds in the Shetlands and Faroes, and it has begun to show its face in Iceland, presumably as a consequence of milder conditions.

It will live in open country but there has to be easy access to cover, which it reaches in short flying dashes, keeping close to the ground. Birdtables must be an important factor in its success as a city dweller. It will eat a wide variety of food and is also undemanding in its choice of nest site. One way and another it is an adaptable bird, and that is the supreme quality required for late-twentieth-century survival.

'The ousel cock, so black of hue, with orange tawny bill,' said Shakespeare (*A Midsummer Night's Dream*), and with blackbirds, unlike robins, the sexes are easily distinguished. The cock bird is a semi-matt black, without the metallic sheen of other black birds like crows. He has a fine orange-yellow bill and eye frame, dark-brown legs and feet. The hen has dark-brown upperparts, a paler throat, and mottled dark-brown underparts with spots, rather like a thrush, indeed she is occasionally mistaken for a thrush. The juveniles are even lighter-coloured than the female, with a touch of rufous-brown in their colouring. Again they have sporty underparts. For their first year, the young males have a blackish bill.

Blackbird plumage is variable, and there is a marked tendency to abnormalities. Most of us will have seen an albino, or part-albino, example. Folklore gives the most graphic explanation for this tendency, that it is the *blackness* which is abnormal. The bird started life as white as snow but, exposed to a particularly fierce winter, took refuge in a chimney, with sooty results. The last two days of January and the first of February are called 'blackbird days' in the Brescia region of Italy, commemorating the days on which the transformation is said to have happened.

A survey which analysed over three thousand occurrences of albinism showed that the six species most commonly affected were blackbird, sparrow, starling, swallow, rook and jackdaw. Except in the case of the swallow, the phenomenon affects birds which tend to lead somewhat sedentary and sociable lives. The

Sunbathing

A partial albino
male Blackbird
living in the artist's garden

Oiling and preening

Female Blackbird brooding

causes are not easily defined: they may have something to do with a dietary deficiency, perhaps associated with a high intake of 'artificial' food offered at birdtables. Certainly albinism appears to be most often noticed in urban and suburban habitats, where birdtable food provides a significant proportion of a blackbird's diet.

Whatever the reason, it is a fact that the blackbird is more prone to albinism, partial or total, than any other species. In the true albino, pigment is completely absent, even the beak, legs and eyes being colourless, but most often the condition is partial, with the plumage revealing a patch of white, or perhaps just one white feather. The extent of the whiteness may vary from season to season, and albino or part-albino young may be produced by normal parents as easily as normal young may be produced by albino parents. An individual may show more white as the years go by. Any feather on the bird may be affected, but the head is particularly prone. One can't help wondering to what extent the white blackbird is at a disadvantage, because at the least it becomes conspicuous and therefore extra vulnerable to predation. But the suburban habitat, while it may be partly responsible for the problem, is at least a relatively protected environment. So perhaps it is a case of six of one and half-a-dozen of the other.

Whiteness is not the only genetic abnormality suffered by blackbirds. Other 'isms' produce varying intensities of reddishness and yellowishness (erythrism and xanthochroism). In our own garden as I write this we have a gloriously honey-coloured blackbird, an example of leucism, where the normal pigment is diluted and paled. Another common plumage abnormality is melanism, where the bird has too much of the dark pigment eumelanin. These melanistic forms have an exaggerated blackness. Pheasants provide the most commonly seen examples of this.

Whatever the colour of our blackbird's plumage, its maintenance is of great importance. At the bird-bath he shows his feathers off to great advantage: the wings outspread, the handsome tail held down at a right angle and fanned out to show its full spread. Even in the depths of winter birds must bathe their plumage frequently as part of the process of keeping their insulating and flying suit in full working order. Bedraggled feathers waste body heat and make for inefficient flying, and in winter lost energy is not easily replaced. So a good deal of time is devoted to bathing and preening. With the tail fanned out sideways, the oil gland over its base secretes oil which is collected by the bill. Then the oil is worked into the plumage systematically, feather by feather, as a dressing and waterproofing material. Bath water is not the only medium in which birds bathe, incidentally. Pigeons, for instance, enjoy rain-bathing, and sparrows and others enjoy dust-bathing. The most curious form is when birds – and blackbirds indulge a great deal – seek out places where ants are swarming and either deliberately place them, crushed, among their feathers, or allow them to swarm all over their passive bodies. Presumably the formic acid ejected by the ants plays some part in feather maintenance.

At certain times as when anting, blackbirds may be approached closely, but they have a tendency to skulk in borders and under bushes. They are seldom far from shelter. Sprightly, active birds, they explore hedge-bottoms and garden borders, mostly at ground level, turning dead leaves, usually with the bill, sometimes with the feet. Under trees and bushes, they toss and turn the crackling leaves, searching for food, sounding as if an army is on the march in the undergrowth: it comes as a surprise when one solitary blackbird reveals itself, only to panic the moment it sees you and scream off in alarm, rattling into safety. On the ground, it both runs and hops, typically moving a few yards then stopping to think. Hunting worms it will sometimes bound across the lawn with a busy hopping motion.

Earthworms are an important part of its diet, so perforce it is an early riser, for while the surface is still damp and dewy the moisture-loving worm will show its face. And the blackbird needs all the sharpness of its eyes to track down the worm. Birds have exceptional sight, of course. Their eyes are much larger than they appear, for only the small cornea is visible, the greater part of the eyeball lying hidden in the skull. In the blackbird, the eyes are located at the side of the head, so they are at their best looking out to each side, the vision ahead being peripheral. Their keenest field of vision is therefore at right angles to our own. And as the eye doesn't move about in its socket, as ours does, the bird must move its head to scan a different angle. In fact it tends to hold its head still, and steam a zigzag course across the lawn, searching; and from each pause position to move away at right angles to investigate something it has seen. When it catches a glimmer of movement at grass-level, it cocks its head in what looks to us exactly like a 'listening' attitude, when in fact it is directing its eye to search the immediate area by its feet. Once it has a grip on the worm, the attitude reverts to one which looks more 'natural' to us, while it engages in the tug-of-war.

Earthworms, insects, spiders, snails, are all grist to the blackbird's mill. Although the song thrush is the bird generally known to seek snails to smash at an anvil, blackbirds (which are also members of the thrush family) can and do break shells to get at the meat inside. In fact the list of species which a blackbird will eat is quite lengthy – including wasps, slugs, lizards, even newts from a garden pond. They'll take flatworms from the undersides of lily leaves in the garden pond, minnows, sticklebacks, small fry of all sorts, even trout. I once had a correspondent who watched a pair of blackbirds catching small fish from a shallow river and wanted to know if she should put fish on the birdtable. I suggested she try it: I've often wondered whether she did, and what the result was. After all, it's no odder than putting out African groundnuts and exotic petshop seeds for the birds. Blackbirds will take a variety of fruit and vegetables as well as all those animals: they'll eat tomato, for instance, and especially in time of drought will be very destructive to fruit. Holly, hawthorn, ivy, cherry, many fruiting and berry-bearing trees and shrubs will attract family parties in late summer and autumn. Later in the year conditions become much harder for them, especially when they must forage when the ground is frostbound and perhaps even covered with snow. Again they are adaptable: a blackbird has been seen enjoying the patch of bare ground uncovered by grey squirrels scratching for seeds.

Home-bred birds remain in Britain for the winter, although there is some movement from the north towards Ireland and southern England. Their numbers are swelled by a considerable influx of continental birds which migrate across the channel. Crossing at night, many have lost their lives by collision with lighthouses, and if they are caught in fog they are especially vulnerable. The skipper of one of the Marine Biological Association's research vessels told me that once he was offshore when a foggy dawn revealed a perfectly calm sea with many land birds drowned in it. In these conditions migrating birds frequently land on boats, or anything else which gives them somewhere to rest.

The wintering visitors stay with us till early spring, when they return south for the breeding season. By this time our own birds may have been singing for a couple of months, and indeed may already have started to nest. The blackbird's song is the first link in the nesting sequence. Of all our resident song birds, I think thrushes are the quality performers, but plenty of people would argue that the blackbird beats all the rest of the thrush family, including our summer visitor the nightingale. And long before the migrants arrive to cheer us with the spring sounds of cuckoo and chiffchaff, thrushes have been warming the drizzly winter days with song. The mistle thrush will perform right from the turn of the year. Not the most melodious but perhaps the loudest thrush, it will often sing in blustery, showery weather, high in a tree, challenging the elements to do their worst; its old country name is 'stormcock'. Its song has something of a hard, aggressive quality by comparison with the song thrush, which has a sweet song, clear and full-bodied, repetitive but full of variety. It lives up to its name, certainly, indulging in a lot of singing – a favourite of the poets, and it is good to be able to record that for once they got their ornithology into line with their imaginations. Browning says 'that's the wise thrush, he sings each song twice over', and indeed it does tend to repeat each phrase twice, sometimes three times. But I think the most poetic, and accurate, rendering is from Tennyson: 'Summer is coming, summer is coming, I know it, I know it, I know it.'

The blackbird performs two different songs, its early morning performance having a very different quality from the evening serenade. At dawn it strikes up in a slightly half-hearted sort of way, with staccato phrasing of short statements, a bit monotonous and building to an anticlimax. But at least it is easy to distinguish from those other two thrushes. And when it comes to perform at the second house, in the evening, you hear why it's widely regarded as being the equal of a nightingale. As the winter months mature into spring, its song improves. Longer and more musical phrasing, a rich and mellow warble, lower in pitch than the song thrush, unforced and full of feeling. If only it could bring itself to a firmer coda – a stronger conclusion – it would be the finest singer of all. Blackbirds don't sing well when the weather is dry and windy, but improve after a good sharp shower of rain. A still, damp evening suits them well. That's when the old saying 'to whistle like a blackbird' – in other words to do something easily – comes into its own, for it certainly seems an effortless affair. 'When the blackbird sings loud and shrill, rain is sure to follow' (Irish weather lore, c1885).

It is not a particularly sociable bird (though on occasion a number might gather at roosting time) but at courting time, in early spring, you may see a number of unsuited males at a communal gathering. On open ground, several males will parade with lowered tails and half-spread wings. Chasing and posturing, they measure their strength against each other, even though there may not be a female in sight. Once paired, they may begin nesting as early as the end of February, the first stage being selection of a site. Unlike the robin, a blackbird will tolerate another pair of its own species nesting nearby, provided food is plentiful. Typically the nest will be a few feet above the ground, in a bush or bramble clump, amongst dense ivy, or in a shrubbery. Often enough they will choose a ledge on a wall or inside an outhouse. Of course they don't always choose wisely; but on an unsuitable site the nest usually comes to grief, found too soon by a small boy, or simply disintegrating because of poor support. Using material brought by the cock, the hen creates a large well-built structure of twigs, leaves, grasses and roots, with quite a lot of moss. These foundations are bound and lined with mud and completed with an inner layer of fine grasses. When the nest is ready the hen lays one egg every day, usually in the early morning, until the clutch of four or five, bluish-green richly freckled with reddish-brown, is complete.

Blackbird's nest—not always well hidden (*Jane Burton*)

This may happen as early as Christmas, often in January and February, although of course the normal laying time is late March and April onwards.

Birds may lay eggs at any time of year, but cold weather and the scarcity of food allow very few winter families to survive. Natural selection will always ensure that most birds nest when food is most freely available. Indeed even the size of the clutch is regulated by the available food: in cold or drought fewer eggs are laid. Conditions may have improved by the time the eggs hatch, but the birds don't have any way of foreseeing this when they lay. First-time breeders also lay fewer eggs. And something which may surprise many people is that farmland and woodland pairs lay more eggs on average than garden birds, because suburban feeding is less satisfactory though it may be generous.

Incubation takes about a fortnight, the brooding mother transferring body heat to the eggs by way of her brood patch. Just sitting on the eggs would be unsatisfactory, because of course a bird's coat of feathers provides very efficient insulation; feathers are designed to keep the body heat *in*. So the hen blackbird has a bare, unfeathered patch on part of her ventral body surface, an area of skin specially supplied with blood vessels, allowing body heat to escape and warm the eggs. When a domestic hen settles on to eggs, you will notice the way she wriggles about, ensuring maximum contact between the eggs and her warm brood patch. Not all birds use this technique. Cormorants, for instance, stand on their eggs, but their webbed feet are highly vascular. I once hand-reared a young cormorant, which used to enjoy balancing on my wrist as if it were a falcon: its pliable feet were quite noticeably warm. Cuckoos don't need to bother with brood patches!

Blackbirds' nests are not particularly difficult to find, so they may suffer from interference. Unless the individuals are tame and well-known to you, they are best left alone to get on with the job, although birds don't desert the nest quite as readily as many people think. An old wives' tale has it that handling the eggs, or for that matter the young, causes birds to desert automatically, but that's not true either. However, the female will be reluctant to leave the nest when the eggs are near to hatching. This reluctance is often interpreted by well-meaning people as evidence of her love for them!

Once hatched, the nestlings are fed by both parents for a couple of weeks. At first they are blind, naked and helpless, with one interest in life – a stomach full of food. When the parent, bringing food, alights on the nest the structure shudders. The response of the chicks is immediate: they open their mouths wide, and gape upwards. The brightly coloured mouths stimulate the parent bird to respond by dropping in food. At the end of the first week, when their eyes open, the chicks are further stimulated by the sight of the arriving adult, although at this stage they will gape hopefully when *anything* moves above them. Only after a few more days do they learn to direct their gape towards the adult, rather than simply upwards. The

Hen Blackbird about to feed
her blind and naked nestlings

parents bring a steady stream of squashed bugs in their bills, and take away the droppings, keeping the nest tidy and clean. As the chicks grow, they begin to show more interest in their surroundings, and it is not too much to say that they begin to enjoy play. Pecking and nudging the nest material and overhanging twigs and leaves, they are already beginning to learn about their world and to evaluate the nest-making and food potential of the materials around them.

To distinguish between instinctive and learned behaviour is difficult, especially as most of the more striking actions in a bird's life appear to the casual observer to be the result of rational thinking. These processes of courting, nest-building, egg-laying, brooding and rearing young are most clearly shown to be instinctive when, for some reason, the sequence is upset. Then the birds are completely thrown off course, and instead of picking up the pieces and carrying on, they must perforce return to square one and start all over again. Should the nestlings be removed from the nest by a marauding squirrel, which is interrupted in its work and abandons them a short distance away, the parent bird, while perfectly capable of picking them up and returning them to the nest, does not do so. The nestlings die. The parents either give up altogether or start courting again, preparatory to building another nest. Mammals are much better organised to deal with this kind of problem. Disturbed at one nest, they will freely move, lock, stock and barrel, and set up home elsewhere to continue rearing the same family.

The young blackbirds leave the safety of the nest when they are nearly two weeks old. As fledglings, with their first flying suit of feathers, they flutter about uncertainly, highly vulnerable to predators and 'rescue' by well-meaning people. The parents are never far away, and when danger threatens they make a special 'chook' call which warns the young to sit tight and play it cool. So don't feel impelled to gather up the stray birds you find in garden borders, even when they tremble their wings and reach up to you with wide-open gapes, asking to be fed. Quite apart from the fact that they are very rarely abandoned, the task of caring for them is demanding. They need almost uninterrupted feeding through the hours of daylight, and constant warmth. The task of returning them to the wild is also time-consuming. But the most powerful reason for not taking the job on is that it is not necessary. Soon enough the juveniles learn to make themselves scarce when trouble looms, and to welcome the parents when they bring food: crouching with wings a-flutter, head outstretched and cheeping, they are charged with energy in the form of fat bugs. Both parents share in the work, and this phase lasts some three weeks. As the days go by the young birds learn to feed themselves by watching their parents' technique. Turning, searching and pecking amongst leaves, discovering the bird table, the young will still display at their parents, demanding food even though they are standing in an ocean of it. But soon you'll see them imitate the parents with a hesitant stab at the table, picking up a morsel – dropping it – picking it up again – until the penny suddenly drops.

By this time the mother may already be starting another clutch of eggs. There is a record of a pair of blackbirds rearing five families in one season, producing at least fifteen, probably sixteen, young. No wonder mortality is so high among young birds: if they all survived to breed, the world would soon be submerged in a carpet of blackbirds! The durability of a well-built blackbird's nest is quite impressive. One nest, built in a well-protected shed, was used six times in three successive seasons. And even when the nest has outlived its original purpose, never to see an egg again, it may provide a home for a toad, or a dining-room for a mouse. In suitably damp situations the mosses used in its construction may continue to grow and draw nourishment from the earthy lining, so that in due course the nest itself becomes a whole new community of plants and insects.

4 BLUE TIT . . . THE ACROBAT

The nearest thing to perpetual motion in the bird world. Small,
stumpy-billed, bull-necked, a vivacious bird with sociable
manners. A birdtable and nestbox addict: anyone who has ever
thrown out a few crumbs or peanuts will know this welcome
garden visitor. The tomtit, or blue tit, has bright blue and
yellow plumage, which immediately sets it apart from the
blacks, browns, reds and greens of the majority of everyday
birds. With a white side to its face, and a white border to the
blue cap, the sulphur-yellow underparts are neatly set off by the
dark centre-line of the belly. Compared with the other titmice
it has a rather short tail. Its voice is not particularly noteworthy:
just a variety of rather uninspiring tsee-tsee sounds. But its
behaviour more than makes up for this lack of musicianship.
Busy and restless, searching every nook and cranny, perching or

hanging at any and every angle, it is always on the lookout for new grounds to explore and exploit. It has dark sides to its character, as we shall see, but a general air of rounded innocence and fun which serves it well in most people's eyes.

It is true that in spring time the blue tit will attack buds. But it's not unique in that, and to make up it eats bucketfuls of insects and larvae. It will eat a variety of seeds, from wheat to beechmast and pine; and, given the chance, sunflower seeds. Above all, it will devour peanuts provided by admiring householders. In autumn, not far from our house, blue tits roam in family parties through the reedbeds at the side of the estuary, eating seeds and insects busily. Like both robin and blackbird, their ancestors lived in woodland and copse; now gardens, hedgerows and orchards suit them very well.

In orchards, most of all, this acrobatic bird is in its element, actively seeking out and destroying, or rather recycling, great quantities of caterpillars, bugs and larvae of all kinds.

> And then the bluecap tootles in its glee,
> Picking the flies from orchard apple tree.
>
> (John Clare, *The Firetail's Nest*)

In 1825 John Clare, our finest naturalist-poet, watched a hen blue tit taking caterpillars from apple-blossom and plum leaves: 'She fetched 120 caterpillars in half an hour.' Since then, other observers have estimated that a pair of blue tits may bring an average of 700 caterpillars a day to their nestlings; an astonishing quantity. Can we doubt that, on balance, blue tits are an asset to any garden or orchard? Unfortunately it's not so easy to decide. For they eat not only the 'bad' insects (ie the ones which don't suit the fruitgrower or forester) but the 'good' ones, too. At least they are not eating the actual trees, and their activities probably cancel out neatly, which is just as it should be; living room assured for blue tits, 'good' and 'bad' insects – all providing food for each other on a long-term basis.

Beekeepers are not entirely fond of blue tits, which like both honey and bees: in some parts of the country tits were known as

bee-birds; they wait at the hive or nest entrance and nobble the bees as they come out. On a cold day, when the insects will be torpid, they may actually enter the hive. Though to most people tomtits appear the most charming and inoffensive of birds, you only need to watch one deal with a bee to think again. It holds the insect down firmly with a foot, and hacks it open with its bill in the style of a bird of prey. In Devon, tomtits were once known as 'hackymals', a direct reference to their devasting technique. They are well able to deal with the poison of the female bee, rubbing the prey against the perch and discharging the venom before eating the meat. Wasps are dealt with in like manner, also being good to eat, except for the sting. However, the blue tits don't always have it their own way; there are records of wasps driving them away from ripening fruit, and blue tits have been seen to be wary of investigating a bone upon which wasps were already feeding. Other birds eat bees and wasps, but even a robin has been seen to discard the sting before crushing the head of a honey bee and swallowing it whole. The honey buzzard is a specialist, probably immune to the venom,

Blue Tit dismembering a bee

but for all that he has close-fitting feathers around his beak and head, possibly as a protective barrier.

Much as they clearly like bees and wasps, the delicacy which we most often see tits enjoying around us is the humble peanut. Although peanuts no longer come at a humble price, they are full of protein and conveniently transported, and will be welcomed so enthusiastically by most garden birds that you will have to offer them in a container which reduces the number of species able to get at them. The Royal Society for the Protection of Birds (see page 121 and save two birds with one cheque by joining the society when you send for the feeding things) produces an excellent peanut dispenser in the form of a wooden box with a mesh base; as the nuts have to be taken from underneath, only the most agile birds can feed. They also offer a spiral wire feeder which can be attached to a window-pane with a suction cup, and though it doesn't hold many nuts it provides great pleasure for people who are housebound. Another useful feeding device is a scrap cage, made of plastic-covered wire. It holds a good quantity of peanuts and will be visited by a procession of tits and finches.

It has to be said that the 'wrong' birds can also learn to take advantage of feeding devices – but even sparrows and starlings have to live! With a bit of luck you can outwit sparrows with a tit bell, the traditional device for offering a mixture of fat and scraps. The Dartmouth Pottery (Warfleet, Dartmouth, Devon) make one which was designed by Robert Gillmor and myself, so it must be good!

Winter is the traditional time for feeding birds, and although I don't see why anyone should lay down the law about it, there doesn't seem a lot of sense in indulging the birds in the summer months, especially as there is a strong possibility that 'artificial' food may cause a lot of distress and some mortality to young birds. Certainly peanuts ought to be withdrawn from the bird larder in spring and early summer, because it is only too easy for a parent bird to stuff a whole nut down a chick's gape, with dire consequences.

A pair of blue tits may bring an average of 700 caterpillars a day to their nestlings (*Stephen Dalton*)

Peanuts are such a useful and pleasurable food to offer birds that it is important to know about their drawbacks. *Salted* peanuts are very bad indeed for birds. One man's meat is another's poison. Many mammals, hoofed animals especially, enjoy salt, but birds do not. Domestic cattle, wild creatures like deer, go for salt, and on the African plains elephants and antelopes will come to specially prepared salt-licks. The trace elements of sulphates, magnesium, iron, phosphorous and so on must help to correct some dietary deficiency. But salt is disastrous for blue tits and garden birds. Their kidneys are not effective at eliminating it. Most birds don't encounter it;

seagoing birds have special arrangements for dealing with it. Blue tits don't, so do please be careful not to offer them salty food. Having said that, it's only fair to add that apart from salty or highly spiced items you can put out almost any food on a birdtable, because the birds themselves will very soon decide what they should or should not eat.

The question of birds' intelligence is a thorny one. So much of what they do appears to be programmed in advance that it may not be easy to concede that they are capable of creative thought. In this connection it is important to remind ourselves that it is as dangerous to regard all blue tits as possessing a single mind as to think of man in that way. We are all different, so are blue tits. The differences may be subtle, and indeed undetectable to us as yet, but they must exist. What evidence is there that birds (let alone people!), have intelligence?

Perhaps it is as well to start by avoiding that particular word, as intelligence is difficult to define ornithologically. But if we think of learning capacity, the ability to adapt behaviour as a result of experience, then birds do have that and benefit from it. We can certainly say that not all bird behaviour is instinctive and inflexible. Like people, they are capable of taking advantage of experience. Young birds know how to fly when they are born. The essential movements of flight are programmed in their brains long before they exercise them. But their performance improves wonderfully after a few circuits and bumps. Their first marriage and their first breeding season may be a disaster, but they usually go on to better things. Birds become used to noises and movements which prove harmless, they take avoiding action in the face of recurring events which serve them ill. Though in many departments they may behave to a strict pattern with little variation, there are others in which they modify their actions to advantage. That, after all, is what survival and evolution is all about.

Tits probably provide the best of all examples of adult bird learning from adult bird with their well-known assaults on the cream in milk bottles on people's doorsteps. The delights of bottled cows' milk were first discovered in 1921 by an enterprising tit near Southampton. In no time at all the habit was imitated by others and the news gradually radiated all over the country. While at first sight it might appear an extraordinary thing for a tit to have learnt, the bottle-opening feat comes well within the compass of their everyday actions. For above all else tits are enterprising and curious animals, always searching in odd nooks and crannies for insects. Their natural haunt is the trunk and branches of a tree, where they examine crevices in bark and look underneath leaves and in the crooks of twigs. In an urban or suburban setting, they search window frames and guttering, prising and investigating any promising dent or orifice. Seen for the first time, a milk bottle represents yet another curious-looking branch of a tree, something to be prodded and scratched in the hope of revealing a fat grub. When that first cardboard milk-bottle-top gave way under attack, the tit continued to investigate, and the creamy milk was the reward. Once rewarded, a lesson is not lost, and the next milk bottle received the same enthusiastic attention.

If there's anything new in the garden or round the house, you can be sure that whereas most animals will be very cautious of approach, tits will be the first to investigate its possibilities. Presented with complicated intelligence tests involving matchboxes with secret doors and latches, tits will soon learn their way to the hidden peanut. But the components of all the required actions are ones which they use in everyday tree-top life.

Some of their antics can be tiresome. When they strip the wallpaper from your room, for instance, you may feel that beguiling air of innocence is hardly feather-deep. Wallpaper tearing is something we hear about mainly in early winter. In the ordinary way blue tits are not specially keen on entering houses, though why this should be the case I don't know, since from such explorer-characters one would have expected

Blue tits roost and nest in dark and secret places (*Stephen Dalton*)

otherwise. Anyway in times when blue tits have enjoyed mild winters and a good breeding season, our thriving British populations may be swelled by a mighty irruption of continental birds which come to join us in September–October and stay for several months. Food supplies come under pressure, and this may be why tits investigate the possibilities indoors. The actual wallpaper stripping is most likely only another version of bark stripping from trees, although one theory suggests that it is a form of play, only indulged in when there is an *abundance* of natural food, allowing spare time.

Not only wallpaper comes under attack. Tits, and other species, will play havoc with newly-puttied windows, presumably enjoying the linseed oil. Certainly they are fond of fat, as anyone who has offered bacon rinds and suet on a birdtable will know.

Blue tits are hole-nesting and roosting birds. For many years they have taken advantage of the enclosed warmth of streetlamps on cold nights, and indeed they will use the light of the lamp to lengthen the day's hunting hours. More normally they roost in tree holes or crevices in buildings. And when it comes to nesting time they use the same sort of secret places. If there is a shortage of sites then they will press an astonishing variety of niches into service, letter-boxes, old cans, bottles and so on. They take to specially provided nest-boxes with relish. As you become more interested in birds, after feeding them by way of birdtables and hanging devices, the next most enjoyable operation is to put up nestboxes. They are very easy to make (construction details are in *The New Bird Table Book*), or you can buy a plywood box from the RSPB (address on p 121).

The hen bird builds the nest, of mosses and grass, lined with stuff like hair, feathers and wool. Put suitable materials in one of those mesh carrot-bags and hang it from the bird table in April and May. You'll find it is much patronised, and not only by tits. The white, speckly-chestnut eggs nestle into the warm lining, and an astonishing number there may be. Anything from seven to fourteen is usual, but up to twenty-four have been recorded in a single nest, though without much doubt this was the result of two females' labours! The hen incubates the eggs for a fortnight, being fed on the nest by the cock bird. Then, for up to three weeks, both parents bring quantities of caterpillars to feed the young.

Usually there is just one brood. Be careful not to disturb the birds when they are nearly fully fledged, because if they 'explode' out into the world too soon they may only be preyed upon. There is a general rule that the ratio of the sexes is about equal in any clutch, but as time goes by more males survive than females. With so many chicks, inevitably some must die in the first week of life. The vigorous chick which stretches and gapes well, and makes most noise, tends to get fed first. The one which holds back is unlikely to survive.

In terms of expectation of life, there is a yawning gap between the age which an individual may reach – one blue tit lived eleven years – and the average lifespan, which is less than a year. Most small birds die in their first few months. If they can fight through to sexual maturity, their prospects are much better. It is all rather sad, but that's the way it has to be, because if all those eggs resulted in birds, which in turn laid more successful eggs, there'd very soon only be enough room in the world for blue tits. So don't begrudge the magpie, or the squirrel, his legitimate prey. Cats are another matter!

5 THE SOCIABLE . . . STARLING

As recently as the last century, the starling was a scarce breeding bird in parts of Britain. Times have changed. Now it is abundant, some would say superabundant. For the starling is not a popular bird; birdtable enthusiasts widely regard it as the bird they would most like to see the last of. It lacks the vital ingredient of cuddly-looking plumpness, the comfortably human characteristics of friendliness and diffidence, which we appreciate; it enjoys a brash, sociable life in which we are not invited to join. Its sheer numbers overwhelm the garden facilities. In short, it is not welcome. It is the victim of its own success. We prefer an underdog to a top dog.

And yet it is an entertaining mimic, a great eater of leatherjackets, earwigs and other 'harmful' bugs, and has a smart, distinctive appearance. The plumage which looks dull black from a distance turns out to be brilliantly glossy in reality, in wintertime star-spangled with tints of green, purple and bronze iridescence. The legs are an attractive reddish-brown, and at the onset of breeding condition the tips of the feathers are spotted with white.

The young birds look thoroughly un-starling-like. In their first juvenile plumage they are grey-brown with a pale underbody and off-white throat, only becoming spotted in their first winter. 'Solitary thrush' was the name given to them in some parts of the country at one time, in the mistaken belief that they were a different species altogether. Even now they are often at first mistaken for rare American visitors when they turn up at coastal bird observatories in late summer.

As young birds they have a particularly boring voice. No one will promote starlings for the Eurovision Songbird Contest, but the adults are at least interesting songsters. They warm up with churrings, clickings, whistlings, one moment musical, the next positively mechanical. Then the song, somewhat under-powered, pours out as a garrulous and rambling warble, larded with clicks, gurgles and whistles. The saving grace is their astonishing versatility in mimicking the calls and songs of other birds, cattle, cats, dogs and people. Many years ago Thomas Bewick noted that starlings are easily tamed, very docile, and quickly learn to whistle tunes 'with great exactitude'. A Scottish poet was a convert.

> Of all the birds whose tuneful throats
> Do welcome in the verdant spring,
> I prefer the starling's notes,
> And think she does most sweetly sing.
> Not thrush, nor linnet, nor the bird
> Brought from the far Canary's coast,
> Nor can the nightingale afford
> Such melody as she can boast.
>
> (Allan Ramsay, *Song*)

Starlings are a highly successful species: everywhere you go

Great flocks of Starlings
perform mass aerobatic
displays before settling
into their roost

Feeding Starlings
move rapidly across grassland,
probing the tussocks for grubs and insects

they are plentiful. One of the requirements for avian success in the seventies is a catholic taste in food, and the starling will duly eat almost anything – insects, seeds, fruits, birdtable scraps. It is quick to find food, quick to move on when the supplies are exhausted and discover new sources. Always ready to move, search and search again. If a colony of flying ants is swarming, starlings will appear from nowhere and hawk them as swallows would, swerving and gliding and taking their fill. If you hang a patent nut-basket, guaranteed to supply tits and greenfinches and discourage the raggle-taggle, the starling will keep trying till it cracks the problem, holding tight to the mesh and eating the nut, or taking it and flying away. Given the chance it has even been known to steal sparrows' eggs and to carry off nestling birds. All in all, the starling is a highly interesting, if not charming, character.

If you take a close look at garden birds you will often find that some of them display abnormalities of the beak, and starlings seem particularly prone. It is not uncommon to see a bird with a down-curved bill as much as a couple of inches long, curlew-like. Such birds seem to manage well enough, although sometimes this must be because they are paid special attention at birdtables, for they find it very difficult to pick up natural food. A bird's bill of course, acts as its hand. The horny sheath is a projection of the jaws, and like a finger-nail it is growing all the time. Normally wear and tear compensate for the rate of growth and the bill remains at a useful operating length; a tool used in nest building, preening and feeding. If damaged, the bill will regenerate, but the process takes time, and the bird must be at a disadvantage meanwhile. Oddly shaped bills are not always caused by an accident; they can result from a genetic abnormality. On the whole it is surprising how little annoyance they seem to cause – though we just don't see the worst-afflicted birds because they don't survive.

There is one aspect of starling life which you can observe in any garden, and it is the key to much of their success. Watch them feeding, and notice that they are all feeding together.

Then maybe one of them decides to go and have a dip in your birdbath. (Every bird garden has a shallow bowl of bathing water, carefully placed with at least six feet of open country round it, to give advance warning of cats.) What happens? Do the other starlings carry on feeding and allow the bather to get on with the job? Not a bit of it. They join in, with much bustle and noise and barracking. And that is a crucial piece of starling psychology. When one feeds, they all feed. When one bathes, they all bathe. Starlings are, above all, gregarious birds. Social birds with a built-in tendency to flock. And one of the characteristics of a flock is this synchronisation of activities. They all fly together, all turn together, all feed together, all drink together, all sing together.

There must be great advantage in subscribing to a social system of this kind. It gives stability to the community. For law and organisation are as valuable to a bird society as they are to the human version. Anarchy is no more successful with starlings than it is with us. Working together as a group, they feed more effectively, since discovery of food by one immediately makes it available to all. Surviving attack by predators, the flock sticks together closely, there being safety in numbers. If a predator has to be tackled, it is easier done with combined forces.

Starlings are even typically sociable with other species. They will fly in and forage on open fields with groups of lapwings, rooks and jackdaws. I've seen them working the tideline of a beach, busily snatching sandhoppers from rotting seaweed, in company with turnstones. They will graze alongside a herd of cattle, taking the insects disturbed by the cows' feet as they swish through the grass – for all the world like cattle egrets. They will do the same with a flock of sheep. But with sheep they have an even more intimate relationship, for they jump right up and find the ticks which parasitise the woolly backs. Perhaps not quite so welcome, they will follow green woodpeckers as they work a lawn for ants, picking up the strays.

On the ground they are busy workers, covering the country with a purposeful walk, sometimes running, sometimes hopping. They feed in close flocks, the individuals evenly spaced, separating the grasses, probing the top layer of the soil, searching out the leatherjackets and other larvae, worms and insects – the teeming animal life of the earth's crust. In spring they create havoc in early cereal crops and in autumn they enjoy ripe fruit. But the balance sheet probably works out on the good side, as they are useful birds to the farmer. They will take caterpillars in quantity, like a titmouse.

In winter the starling depends heavily on leatherjackets (the larvae of crane-flies) during the mild spells which favour them, and in colder conditions looks for grain, and to a lesser extent beetles and snails. But the bird is a supreme opportunist, taking advantage of whatever is most freely available at a given time, thus surviving conditions which test other small birds to their limits.

The most spectacular starling activity comes at bedtime. After what we've seen of its behaviour so far it is no surprise that it indulges in communal roosting. Birds which spend the day together roost together.

> High on the topmost branches of the elm
> In sable conversation sits the flock
> Of social starlings . . .
>
> (Hurdis, *Favourite Village*)

Towards sunset, the foraging garden-parties of starlings fly off to join others. Following well-defined flight paths, perhaps covering as much as thirty miles, the groups coalesce into enormous flocks: a rush-hour in reverse, with countless thousands making their purposeful way to the chosen rest-place. Reed beds, rhododendron thickets, woods, shipyards, city centres all serve their purpose. The build-up begins in mid-June, but reaches a peak much later in the year, after our home-bred birds are joined by a great access of immigrants from the continent.

When the birds reach the vicinity of the roosting area there will often be a spectacular flying display. Dense clouds of starlings fill the sky, sweeping back and forth, changing patterns and densities on a mighty scale. It seems that these displays help to locate the roost-site and also act like a navigation mark to assist the incoming parties in making a correct landfall. High winds or rain cut short the performance, but even in these conditions the incoming flocks mark the spot long enough to guide in the next squadron, then funnel down to roost leaving the newcomers to take over the signalling. On a good night the swooshing, rocketing and funnelling of massed swarms of starlings in these aerial firework displays is one of the most exciting natural events to be seen anywhere, at any time.

As the seemingly endless stream of black rockets funnels down, each individual flies in to land at its own bedside. Whether it is to grasp the stem of a reed or the twig of an elm or a ledge of the Bank of England, each has its chosen perch. As in all small birds, a starling's hind toe is opposed to the others and the flexor tendons are so arranged that when the bird relaxes, its grip is tightened, a comfortable arrangement which ensures that the bird does not fall out of bed the moment it goes to sleep. But before sleep it joins its fellows in singing the evening chorus, a volume of sustained twittering which rises even above the noise level of city traffic. Suddenly the singing will stop, almost as though some sound-man had pulled out a plug: then just as suddenly start again. Like the aerial evolutions, which involve mass changes of course seeming to invite multiple collisions, these instant effects are more apparent than real. In fact we are back to the old familiar pattern. When one changes course, they all change course. And they follow suit so quickly that the action appears, or sounds, instantaneous. This truth can be demonstrated by looking at a piece of film showing the 'instant' manoeuvre, then re-running it as a slow-motion 'action replay'. It is easy to spot the way an individual changes course, to be followed first by those nearest it and in turn by the rest of the flock as the message is passed on within a fraction of a second.

The practice of using city-centre buildings as roosting places

Starlings roosting on the ledges of the Admiralty Arch, Trafalgar Square, London. Each to his personal perch (*Eric Hosking*)

is a relatively recent departure for starlings, dating back to the turn of the century. The first known location was Nelson's Column in Trafalgar Square, which is still well and truly operational. A well-established roost may, over a period of years, become home for anything up to fifty thousand individuals. One of the prime requirements is shelter from wind and rain, and the birds go for tall structures with an abundance of ledges, sills and the sort of ornamentation which produces eaves and cornices. A row of sculptured worthies sheltering in recessed niches serves very well. Modern buildings of the slab-sided concrete and glass variety are despised by starlings, a judgement in which they are not alone! These sheltered roosts represent havens of warmth and safety. Indeed, if the birds get half a chance they will choose sites which offer additional warmth, such as ventilation outlets, or industrial cooling towers. On occasion, though, their preference for industrial

Starlings will nest almost anywhere, but a tree-hole is the typical site (*Stephen Dalton*)

zones can be their undoing. Thick fog in mid-winter may produce 'smog' conditions, and at times starlings have come to grief and been found asphyxiated in the streets. One record tells of ten thousand birds which died in this way on the night of 15 January 1959, having flown into dense smog over the Mersey estuary on the way to their roost. As they fell into the river, the current carried them down and cast them ashore.

Starling roosting habits are all very well, tidy, cosy and resourceful, unless you happen to live in their shadow. The sheer weight of numbers breaks branches, the sheer quantity of droppings kills trees and fouls buildings with a barely tolerable mess. The smell becomes revolting. But it's an ill wind that blows no good. Cast your eye along those thickly-encrusted ledges, and here and there the odd nitrogen-loving elderberry will be thrusting out of a crevice, imported as a seed in a starling stomach and voided into the night to take root and enjoy a guano-rich environment.

After all the evidence of an extremely social life, it comes as something of a surprise that for breeding starlings choose some privacy. Adaptable to the last, though, they will nest almost anywhere, from a pile of stones to a blue tit's nestbox. Normally choosing holes in trees or buildings, they will cheerfully dispossess a woodpecker and take over its newly-excavated nest cavity. If the entrance hole of a nestbox is big enough to permit entry, you may be sure that far and away the most likely occupant will have star-spangled plumage and a talent for rude song and mimicry. It is the unmated male which builds the untidy nest of straw, lined with feathers or leaves and moss. Successfully paired, the hen produces at least half a dozen pale bluish-white eggs. The season begins round about mid-April. Both sexes incubate, though only the hen is on watch at night. The young are fed by both sexes for about three weeks.

After they have left the nest one of the most familiar summer sights is of family starling parties, soon joining forces with other families, building into wandering gangs which swoop about, searching for food. The sociable bird is back with its mates.

6 THE OPPORTUNIST . . . GULL

In Britain we have well over a dozen different species of gull, some of them obscure enough to delight any rarity-hunting birdwatcher. But one of them has the distinction of being the best-known of all seabirds. One of the hardy annuals in broadcasting jokes, at least among the public, has been that the BBC possesses but one gramophone record of 'the seagull's' voice, trotted out on any occasion when the atmosphere of the sea is required. In fact there are umpteen recordings of gull calls, but the typical alarm cry of the herring gull serves better than any other sound to create an instant mind-picture of the sea, or more strictly the sea coast. Quite apart from its evocative call, the gull's white plumage and strong, graceful flight mark it out as one of the very few birds which almost everyone can identify, however meagre their interest in the subject.

The herring gull, and its smaller cousin the black-headed gull, are the two commonest species (the common gull is separate and not particularly common). These are the ones most often seen in seaside towns and, nowadays, many other towns and cities.

They are easily distinguished apart. The herring gull has grey upperwing surfaces with black tips terminated by a white spot, flesh-coloured legs and feet, and a yellow bill with a striking red spot. The black-headed gull has a chocolate-brown head (!) in the breeding season, and its bill and legs are red. In winter the head loses the all-over chocolate, but retains a black flash behind the eye. The juveniles of both species are a dusky mottled brown or grey, and perhaps at this stage it's best to opt gracefully out of writing about gull identification, because the variety of plumages in both adult and juvenile is not something to go into lightly. Apart from the black-backed gulls, the herring and black-headed are far and away the most likely everyday gulls. A very crude division would have the herring as the typical gull of coast and estuary, whereas the black-headed is a bird of inland waters. But there is considerable overlap.

Both species have increased their numbers enormously within this century. Herring gulls have always been abundant, but are at present undergoing an explosive increase. They breed all round the coast of the British Isles, and even in some inland areas, mainly in Ireland, where they colonise lakes and bogs. In Cornwall they have taken to china-clay pits. The rate of increase may be realised if we just look at the island of Steepholm, in the Bristol Channel. In the thirties there were 700 breeding pairs, in 1949 the figure was 1,250, and in 1956 it had risen to about 3,600. That increase is typical of the gull's success all round the coast and it adds up to a staggering population. The cause is easy enough to establish. These birds are scavengers by trade, and they have benefited hugely by exploiting the waste products of man. Not so very long ago they patrolled beaches for tideline casualties, then they tidied the offal and waste from the fishing grounds and shore-based fishing communities, but their breakthrough came with the growth of rubbish dumps and sewage farms, and even the handouts of holiday tourists and retired, lonely, seaside residents.

Black-headed gulls nest in colonies inland as well as on the coast: on sand-dunes and slacks, marshes and saltings, freshwater marshes and rushy loch-sides. The nest is a scruffy structure of any available vegetation, sometimes nothing much at all, just a scraped saucer-shape on the ground. Once these gulls were much esteemed for food, and a nesting colony on a property was regarded as a valuable asset. Reeds and rushes were cut away in the autumn to prepare a welcome ground for the returning birds in the spring. Young birds were collected in great numbers, the gentry assembling to see the sport, and subsequently to enjoy the feasting, patronised by bishops and nobility. Thomas Bewick tells of gulls fetching five shillings a dozen, and of £60-worth being collected in a few days – a princely sum in the first part of the nineteenth century.

Herring gulls have been exploited more for their eggs than their meat, and still are to a certain extent. Like the black-headed gulls, they nest mainly in colonies, but on coastal sites, cliff-top ledges and the grassy slopes of small islands.

In the early spring the birds congregate at courting grounds, where pairs stand about and unpaired birds trumpet their suitability. The males lower their heads, beak on throat, and croon. They snatch at bits of grass, and just as impulsively drop them again. Other males, accepting the challenge, behave in similar fashion. They approach each other, then back away, trying their weight. Several males may group together, and status and rank slowly emerge. There may even be fights and a few lost feathers. The females may not appear to be involved, but in due course birds make attachments, marked by formal promenades, where they bow and circle each other, bow again and finally sit face-to-face, in what looks very much like an old-tyme-dance performance. Over a period of time the pair-bond is formed and consummated, with much excitement and noise, billing and begging. The large nest is comfortably built by both sexes of whatever vegetable material is available – grass, seaweed, heather – and is made complete with three, sometimes four, speckled olive eggs.

These nests are mainly built on cliff ledges and island slopes, but over the last sixty years or so there has been what at first sight is a striking departure from this norm. Herring gulls (and, to a lesser extent, kittiwakes, and lesser black-backs) took to nesting on the roofs and amongst the chimney-tops of buildings. Although the first records date back to 1910, the phenomenon really became established in the twenties, in the south-west, spreading by the thirties to the south-east, and subsequently to the east coast and to Wales and Scotland. When 'Operation Seafarer' counted the seabirds of the British Isles in 1969–70, there were about 1,300 gulls' nests on buildings. And although this number represents an insignificant proportion of the herring-gull population – most of them still nesting on traditional sites – the venture has had a considerable impact on some people.

Being colonised by herring gulls is something of a traumatic experience. The birds can be aggressive in defence of the nest territory, and if your front drive happens to come within those bounds then they will divebomb you without mercy. In Newquay, Cornwall, where the habit has been long established, people have actually lost blood in these battles. So they can be awkward neighbours. And of course many people regard their natural processes as dirty habits especially when the droppings fall on their newly-washed status symbol. In Brixham car park it is well established, incidentally, that blue cars are bespattered more than those of other colours. Genteel resorts like Torquay have for years been perplexed by the problem. Anxious to rid the town of muck-producing birds, the council have toyed with solutions ranging all the way from egg-collecting to shooting, none of which can possibly work; they resolutely avoid the real cause of the 'problem' which is, of course, the availability of easy feeding at rubbish tips, augmented by fish offal and the handouts of sympathetic visitors and gull-loving residents.

The spectacle of ignorance fighting the gulls of the world is not enlightening. The most amusing 'solution' was the suggestion that boys should be paid to collect the seagulls' eggs. Quite apart from the fact that not a few boys would inevitably have ended at the bottom of the cliffs, the removal of a gull's egg simply stimulates the female to lay another. The female gull will, rather like the domestic hen, continue to lay until she sees the right number of eggs in the nest before she goes broody. In fact the eggs are very good to eat, and if the proposal had been to institute a form of farming it would have made some sense.

One method of control which is being tried at the moment on Skomer Island, in Pembrokeshire, is to prick the eggs but leave them in the nest. Since this effectively kills the embryo but occupies the parents' time so that no other clutch is attempted, the hope is that the island population may be controlled over a period of years. But success in this type of operation would be difficult to achieve in an area like Torbay, where the nests are not easy to reach and where, in any case, food is the controlling factor and there is no shortage of 'outside' gulls to fly in and reap the benefit.

When the eggs hatch, the nestlings only remain within the nest's confines for three or four days. On the traditional breeding grounds they then find their way to the nearest cover, the shade of bracken or a rock crevice. But up on the rooftops we have the curious spectacle of young birds on the eaves, circumnavigating the chimney pots and strutting in the gutter, waiting for the periodic arrival of the parents with food for regurgitation. As time goes by they play with any bits of twig or pieces of slate which lie about, and they run up and down the roof-slopes, flapping their wings and preparing for take-off. There is no doubt that they make a lot of noise and a lot of mess. Nor is there any doubt that in their role as scavengers they tidy up a lot of mess. And they bring colour and interest to a lot of lonely lives. Even in central London, these enterprising birds have established a stronghold in, of all places, the Regent's Park Zoo. There they have taken over an artificial 'cliff' conveniently placed alongside the seabird aviary, so they have

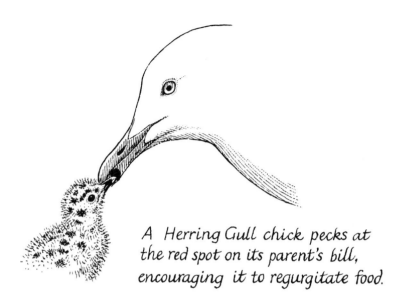

A Herring Gull chick pecks at the red spot on its parent's bill, encouraging it to regurgitate food.

the stimulus of an existing 'colony' of gulls and other seabirds. Doubtless they will breed on the rooftops of the metropolis, and after all from the bird's point of view the ledges and slopes of those buildings are only another version of the more usual cliff slopes. What really attracts them in the first place is the food, there's no shortage of nest sites.

They are not choosy in their attitude to food. Scavenging is their main preoccupation, but they will hunt mice, small birds and rabbits, hawk for flying insects and, when they get the chance, steal from man. Leave a fish-box unattended for a few minutes on a quay and the gulls will move in, just as freely as they'll take your sandwiches. One is said to have entered a restaurant and flown off with a fillet of cod, which it promptly found too heavy and dropped on to the street below. That was a mistake, but at other times gulls will drop cockles or hermit crabs deliberately from a height on to pavements or promenades, in order to break the shell and get at the juicy meat within.

Another piece of gull behaviour is often seen on places like playing fields and water meadows, when rain has left them soaked. The gulls find a sopping patch and mark time on it, trampling up and down, encouraging creatures like worms to come to the surface. For the job the gull foot, rather like a duck's paddle, is very well designed. Much the same thing happens on the seashore, black-headed gulls in particular specialising in 'stationary puddling' in shallow pools, picking off the small marine worms and molluscs which are swirled to the surface. Perhaps gulls hunt cockles this way, too. You may try it for yourself easily enough, next time you are on a sandy beach at low water of spring tides. Pat the sand with your palms to make a quicksand. This is quite an effective way of discovering what shellfish are just under the surface.

Seabirds such as gulls have a special problem to overcome in that they are bound to ingest a certain amount of sea water with their food. This means that salt gets into their bloodstream. As we have seen with bluetits, this can have disastrous effects on a bird's health, since their kidneys are inefficient at eliminating the salt. Marine species have specially developed nose glands, located in their skulls. The function of this gland is quite specific, indeed it only works when it is required for the job. It transfers any salt in the blood to a tube system which trickles the salt, in a highly concentrated solution, down the beak right to the tip of the bill. And once it is there it just drips off, like a drip on the end of your nose. If you've ever sat and watched seabirds for a while, gulls or cormorants for instance, or if you've ever had an oiled-up guillemot in the house, you'll know exactly what I mean. The bird will be sitting quietly, digesting the last meal, and every now and then it will shake its head, and away flies a drip of concentrated sodium-chloride solution.

Gulls indulge in roosting flights, though not on the scale of starlings. They may often be seen enjoying an evening thermal in suitable weather conditions, rising steadily in the warm air and swirling about in large flocks. Sociable birds, too, they roost together outside the breeding season on estuary waters, sheltered bays, lakes, islands and such like secluded places. They prefer to gather together in floating rafts, and if they are feeding inland they will converge in large numbers on the nearest reservoir at dusk.

7 SPARROW . . . THE MESSMATE

The house sparrow is not by any means the commonest bird in Britain, but there are said to be nearly ten million for all that. And sometimes the entire lot seem to be in the garden, terrorising the rightful inhabitants. However, no judgement could be more unfair than that, for the sparrow is nothing if not faithful, and its home-loving tendencies are strongly towards sharing that home with you and me. Having chosen its home, it stays with it, apart from its annual holiday to the cornfields. So whether we like it or not – and on the whole we do not – the sparrow lives with us and by courtesy of us.

Probably this is the best-known bird. Yet birdwatchers dismiss it as a 'small brown bird' of no great interest, as they set off for the sewage farm to look for a newly-arrived and thoroughly lost American wader. But even the dull browniness of the plumage is the result of living in grimy cities. In a garden suburb or in the country, it is a subtly coloured bird. The grey crown of the cock caps a chestnut-brown plumage, streaked with black. It has white cheeks and a black throat: not gaudy, but a striking bird nevertheless. It will only be confused with its close relative the tree sparrow, who has a chocolate crown and a double white wing bar, and is much less addicted to human company. Female house sparrows, and the young ones, are less chestnut in colour and lack the grey crown and single white wing bar of the adult male.

Sparrows are sociable, gregarious birds. They have thrown in their lot with man in a very close and long-standing relationship. Long years ago, when men first broke and tilled the soil to produce cereal crops, the sparrows moved in to help eat the seeds. And they have stayed with us ever since. They are parasitic on us, sharing in the fruits of our labours in cultivation and urbanisation. They eat at the same table, in effect, and are our messmates – commensal species, whose success story runs parallel with our own. When men desert an unprofitable farm or a remote island, the sparrow very shortly leaves as well. But where there is cultivation or free food, there is a sparrow. One of the most widely distributed land birds, you'll find it as comfortably at home in Moscow as in Paris, and as an introduced species it flourishes all the way from New York to Buenos Aires and Sydney.

Enjoying the farmer's corn, it soon made sense for the sparrow to share his house as well, so it moved in and nested conveniently close to the dining table. When the poultry were fed, the sparrows joined in. The warmth and safety of buildings suited very well, so sparrows flourished as man flourished. And as villages grew into towns and cities, sparrows quickly became accustomed to the new scene and the new possibilities. Since the main transport vehicle was the horse, vast quantities of straw and grain were available, and sparrows took their share.

With easy pickings all year round, there was never any need to indulge in dangerous activities like migration. Sparrows

became sedentary birds enjoying an easy life. Yet nobody loves them the way they love robins. Sparrows live with us, but we have never really become friends. Farmers don't like them because of their appetites and householders don't like them because they hog the birdtable. Even in folklore they have a bad image. When the cross was being prepared for Christ, swallows carried away the nails in an effort to delay the crucifixion; but the sparrows promptly brought them back, to curry favour. And in Russia they say the sparrow is an unwelcome guest, whose entry into a cottage foretells trouble. As a punishment for its sins its legs were fastened together by invisible bonds, since when it has been unable to run, and must always hop. Horrid thought.

It is hardly surprising that sparrows have been persecuted. When the farmer's wife put down corn for the pigeons and poultry she begrudged the share taken by the sparrow, from whom she got nothing in return except a lot of noisy chirrups. The eighteenth-century French naturalist Count de Buffon summed up the general attitude to the sparrow: 'It is extremely destructive, its plumage is entirely useless, its flesh indifferent food, its notes are grating to the ear, and its familiarity and petulance disgusting.' Only John Clare had a good word to say for it, and indeed he often paid cash he could ill spare to 'tyrant boys', buying liberty for captives.

> And chirping sparrows dropping from the eaves
> For offal kernels that the poultry leaves
> Oft signal calls of danger chittering high
> At skulking cats and dogs encroaching nigh.
> (John Clare, *Rural Morning*)

William Cowper writes in a style more likely to be welcomed by the farmer:

> The sparrow, meanest of the feathered race,
> His fit companion finds in every place,
> With whom he filches the grain that suits him best,

Flits here and there, and late returns to rest.
And whom if chance the falcon makes his prey,
Or hedger with his well-aimed arrow slay,
In no such loss the gay survivor grieves,
New love he seeks, and new delight receives.

The last line is actionable, since in reality the sparrow is a faithful bird, the pair bond being particularly strong. Be that as it may, all men's hands were turned against the thieving brown bird. But the sparrow is a tough cookie. In its time it has suffered onslaught from stones, lead shot, poison and every known trapping device, but it has proved impossible to exterminate. As recently as the last war the Ministry of Agriculture appealed to patriotic Britons to destroy sparrows nests, in order to lessen their effects on the harvest, but although plenty of small boys wrecked every nest they could lay hands on, whether or not it belonged to a sparrow, the bird war was lost before it began. However hard you try you can't defeat sparrows. Hit as hard as you like, they just bob up for more. As long as there's food and a warm safe building nearby, they will be there to enjoy them. Best to learn to live with them.

In fact they sustained a temporary setback with the invention of the internal combustion engine. With the decrease in town-stabled horses, they inevitably suffered from the loss of feed-corn. They are still less common in city centres than they were at the turn of the century. But as one door closed another opened, and with the rise of suburbia and gardens the town sparrows flourished again. As skilled free-loaders they will enjoy lunchtime sandwich ends in the city and birdtable food in the suburb. In winter, the time of greatest difficulty for most birds, our sparrows may even be better off because this is the time when people are most generous with their handouts.

They are tough customers at the birdtable, scattering food

House sparrows thrive where people thrive, all the way from Moscow to New York and Sydney (*Stephen Dalton*)

about in a tiresome manner, and ousting all non-sparrow competition. Tending to operate in pugnacious gangs, they terrorise other small birds and take what they want by virtue of aggressiveness and sheer numbers. Thrusting and showing their muscle, they sweep the dunnocks and chaffinches and tits out of the way. What can be done about it? Not much, but we may take advantage of one of their characteristics, at least for a short respite. They are cocky birds, and impudent: yet they are at the same time cautious by nature, suspicious of anything new. So food placed in a different position may be left free for other species for a while. Putting offerings in several different places may help, too. A novel food basket or bag will be safe from their attentions for a few days, though they will always win through in the end. Less than ten years ago they were foiled by hanging wire-mesh nut baskets of the sort designed for the acrobatic tits and much used by greenfinches. The sparrows showed interest in them and fluttered alongside ineffectively, but failed to get a grip on the mesh – then hung about to pick up any pieces of nut which fell to the ground. As the years went by they learnt to grasp the side of the basket and pick out the nuts in greenfinch fashion. Now this habit is widespread, another example of the learning ability so strikingly demonstrated by the blue tits with their milk bottles. (Incidentally, many other species now enjoy stolen milk.) One of the astonishing successes in garden bird-feeding has been the way in which a previously uncommon garden bird, the siskin, has since 1963 taken to eating peanuts from hanging mesh bags, a habit first observed in Surrey which has been steadily spreading from the south-east as the message is passed from bird to bird.

A device which has beaten most sparrows so far is a suspended wooden box giving access to its nuts only through a grill across the bottom face. This is no problem for the tits, but sparrows, which have learnt to grip and work at nuts from a vertical position, are less keen on hanging upside-down. However, it's only a matter of time before they solve this puzzle, and indeed there have already been records of isolated individuals extracting nuts from a hovering position under the box, and others who have begun to land and grip while upside-down. Such versatile performers, who take seeds from seed-heads in the manner of a goldfinch, work over a tree like a woodpecker, and like a flycatcher hawk for flying insects, are pretty well invincible.

Most of us will have fed crumbs to sparrows while picnicking in public parks, or at outdoor cafés where they congregate. And apparently at factories where bright lights are kept on for the night shift, sparrows take advantage at night of crumbs left over from the tea-break. A similar well-lit all-night cafeteria service is enjoyed by pigeons at railway stations in London. In much the same way house martins and swallows may hawk well after dusk if a bright outdoor lamp attracts flying insects.

The sparrows' feeding pattern is to forage in non-territorial gangs, cleaning up wherever there are easy pickings. They may be found on farms, gardens, parks, and typically in such places as weedy wasteland of the kind associated with railways and dockside installations. Their rough-and-ready tactics are no problem at most of these places, but in gardens they may be considered a nuisance. Their inclination to destroy flower buds in spring is an example. With a special interest in yellow crocus, they will strip off the petals and scatter them about in a manner calculated to annoy any gardener. The only special significance in the choice of these flowers is that after red, yellow is the colour birds tend to go for when they are searching for insects and nectar; doubtless if a red crocus existed they would prefer it.

As a sociable bird with a taste for colonial living, the sparrow has no need for a highly-developed musicality. It does not have to sing in order to lay claim to a territory, since it shares its territory with its mates. And they operate as a gang, taking what they want when they want it. So their song is undistinguished – a variety of cheerful chirps and splutters, with the occasional musical phrase creeping in as if by mistake.

Freed from the constant necessity of proclaiming and

defending territory, sparrows have spare time: they enjoy a highly sociable atmosphere in the local club. Rarely travelling very far, they hardly even bother to fly with more than utilitarian skill. For a sparrow, flying is a useful facility which allows it to get from A to B. It flies straight and does not waste time in the air; no swoopings or acrobatics or joy-rides. About the only time it will show its maximum speed is when it catches sight of a butterfly ripe for the taking. But at the chosen recreation ground it will hop about, flicking its tail, busy doing nothing much and chirping to its friends. In my parents' garden pond a group of them will fly in to bathe in the shallow puddle held by the leaf of a water lily, and perhaps take a tadpole on the side. Sparrows are dust-bathers, too, enjoying a dried-out puddle on a dirt road, scraping and scratching, wriggling and throwing showers of dust over their backs, all part of the duty of feather maintenance. There is an extraordinary account of a gang of sparrows which used the sugar bowls in a works canteen for bathing. They settled into the sugar bath just as if it were a dust bowl, wriggling and wing-flicking and throwing

House Sparrow dust-bathing

the dry sugar all over the table. It sounded very much in character for a works-outing sparrow party.

At courting time, not surprisingly, the spadger indulges in a good deal of noisy squabbling and skirmishing. But it is an unimpressive affair from the watcher's point of view. Several cock birds may hop around an apparently uninterested female, beaks up, tails up and wings dusting the ground, chirping enthusiastically. The 'bored' hen delivers the occasional half-hearted peck. And then the whole thing breaks up when everyone disperses in an anticlimax. Doubtless the action then continues, in privacy, and quite right too.

In keeping with their rather cavalier attitude to life, the sparrows waste no time on a sophisticated nest. The happy home is a disgrace. Built in any available hole around the house, the one certain thing is that it won't be far from the food supply. As I write, the sun has gone down and our local sparrows are clattering home to find their way into the roof cavity through several easy entrances in our dilapidated eaves. First thing tomorrow morning, along with the starlings that share the roof with them, they will wake us up by stamping above our heads. The nest site may be ill-concealed, but it will almost certainly be above reaching-height, and it will be surprisingly difficult to get at. But it will be a scruffy affair, unlikely to reach the pages of the bird edition of *Ideal Home*. The best you can say about it is that it provides a home for eggs and chicks.

Struggling off the ground lugging a piece of string or straw half-a-dozen times as long as himself, the sparrow throws together a large untidy domed structure of hay and straw, with a side entrance leading to an inner chamber lined with feathers or wool. Offer it feathers or the combings from your dog's coat and it will gratefully accept. Sparrows are glad enough to opt out of building a nest at all: given half a chance to take over a blue tit's nestbox or a house martin's nest they will display all the ruthlessness of their species. House martins frequently suffer, bullied unmercifully and driven from their beautifully built

'A large untidy domed structure of hay and straw' (*R.K.Murton*)

mud nests under the eaves. It is possible to defend your martins from these attacks by using a series of strings hung across the nest entrance, weighted with steel nuts. The martins are able to fly in to their nests at a steeper angle than the sparrows, so the take-over is frustrated. More details of this technique can be had from Nerine Nurseries, Brookend, Welland, Worcs, who supply very successful artificial house-martin nests.

House sparrows lay anything from three to five greyish-white eggs, spotted with dark grey or brown. Starting in May, they raise as many as three broods which will take them through to August. While they are raising young, the parents roost at the nest, but later the family will join the gang and enjoy social roosting, perhaps in a dense ivy bush or a well-grown evergreen. Wherever it is, it won't be far from the nest site. Indeed, apart from the autumn raiding parties which take them to the nearest cornfields, the sparrow gang will spend their whole lives within a few hundred yards of the home they share with you and me. But we have to bear in mind that the average expectation of life is less than a year. Even if a young bird manages to reach its first birthday, its expectation will only increase to 21 months. But if it can avoid cats, small boys and sparrow hawks, the longer it lives the greater is its expectation, and the exception may live for as many as eleven years. For a small bird, that's a lot of living.

8 SWALLOW ... SUMMER VISITOR

As the cuckoo is the voice of spring, so the swallow is the visible herald of summer: a joyous bird, welcomed wherever it goes for its sweet song and masterful flying displays. As it perches on a telegraph pole, its glossy blue plumage is set off by the chestnut throat and white underparts. An elegant bird, slim body with narrow pointed wings and forked tail, the two outer feathers trailing; not to be confused with its near relative and flying companion the house martin, which has white underparts from chin to tail, and which shows a striking white rump as it twists and turns in the air — no tail streamers, either. And the house martin builds its nest under the eaves on the outside wall of the house, whereas the swallow prefers to go indoors.

One swallow maketh not summer ... (anon): well perhaps not, but the first swallow brings a lift to the heart. In Cornwall the old custom was to leap into the air on sighting the first in spring, and that seems as sensible a way as any to mark the event. The main arrival of swallows is in mid-April, but early ones have been seen in the first week of February. At first they make for water meadows and marshes, where there is a chance of early insects to refuel them after the long journey from Africa. And one of the causes of the decline in swallow populations may be man's regrettable tendency to drain and reclaim marshes, sometimes in the sacred name of water conservation, a topsy-turvy performance if considered in the light of the fact that marshes, with all their teeming life, are the natural version of man's sterile reservoirs.

Swallows spend much of the day in flight, but will settle freely enough on posts, wires and rooftops. They associate not so much with man as with the animals he keeps, profiting in various ways from the insects which domestic animals support. So the swallow is most at home in the vicinity of farms and stables. It is in the warmth and safety of cowsheds and outhouses, stables and barns, that it chooses to build its nest. Perched on an open joist or rafter, it may be a few feet from the beast which in its daily grazing disturbs the insects the swallow collects, and in its daily pat-making provides a sympathetic environment for the production of yet more insects. So there is a harmonious relationship between the cow in its stall and the swallow family up in the roof.

Originally the swallow bred in the caves of mountain and sea cliff, but nowadays there are more buildings than caves. Since buildings provide exactly the right sort of nest site, and what's more they tend to be closer to the source of food, their colonisation by swallows has worked well.

Individuals return to the same nest site year after year. Their young will return to the same neighbourhood to find a site for themselves. When I restored a derelict farmhouse once the saddest part was when the swallow which had previously nested in a bedroom found that his entrance was blocked by new glass in a window. For several days it continually flew up to the

87

Swallow drinking in flight

window and sought vainly for a way in. The room now boasted
a ceiling and freshly-painted walls, so we hardened our hearts
and shut the bird out; he had to find a new site in the barn,
where we knew there was plenty of room. But I remember very
well how keenly it demonstrated its longing to get in to that
bedroom.

The one requirement for the nest site is that there should be
something to support the structure; perhaps a joist or interior
wall-top, or maybe just a nail or peg. One more important
thing seems to be that the swallow likes to build up *against*
something, a partition, wall or roof-lining.

> The swallow wheels his circling flight,
> And o'er the water's surface skims;
> Then on the cottage chimney lights,
> And twittering chants his morning hymns.
>
> (John Clare, *Summer Morning*)

This habit seems not so common now, but at one time
swallows were much addicted to building in disused chimneys.
Indeed they were called 'chimney swallows' until
comparatively recently. Gilbert White says 'Here and there a
bird may affect some odd, peculiar place, as we have known a
swallow build down the shaft of an old well; but in general
with us this *hirundo* breeds in chimneys; and loves to haunt those
stacks where there is a constant fire, no doubt for the sake of the
warmth. Not that it can subsist in the immediate shaft where
there is a fire; but prefers one adjoining to that of the kitchen,
and disregards the perpetual smoke of that funnel, as I have
often observed with some degree of wonder.'

The nest is constructed of wet mud, plastered up layer by
layer into a saucer shape and held together with straw and hair.
When it is dry, the interior is lined with grasses and feathers.
The building job poses one real problem for the swallow. It is
by nature a bird of the air, content to perch high up, reluctant
to risk the dangers of ground level. But to collect nest mud,
both would-be parents must land. Once down, it is painfully

Swallow arriving at nest with food for young (*Eric Hosking*)

obvious how ill-at-home they are. With short legs designed more to tuck away and reduce air-flow than to assist in actual locomotion, they shuffle about and scoop up beakfuls of sticky mud. In very dry summers it is a kindness to tip a couple of bucketfuls of water over some dusty corner of the yard or road to save martins and swallows the labour of travelling great distances to find mud. But do it somewhere where there is plenty of open space all round, so that cats can't scoop up the swallows instead of the swallows scooping up mud. If they find it impossible to get wet mud they will make use of an old house-martin's nest, or possibly take over the saucer-type nest abandoned by blackbirds or sparrows, which tend to build indoors in suitable swallow places.

From mid-May onwards the hen will incubate four or five white eggs, spotted reddish-brown. And Gilbert White gives a charming description of their introduction to the world outside the chimney:

> The swallow . . . brings out her first brood about the last week in June, or the first week in July. . . . First, they emerge from the shaft with difficulty enough, and often fall down into the rooms below: for a day or so they are fed on the chimney-top, and then are conducted to the dead leafless bough of some tree, where, sitting in a row, they are attended with great assiduity, and may then be called perchers. In a day or two more they become flyers, but are still unable to take their own food; therefore they play about near the place where the dams are hawking for flies; and when a mouthful is collected, at a certain signal given, the dam and the nestling advance, rising towards each other, and meeting at an angle; the young one all the while uttering such a little quick note of gratitude and complacency, that a person must have paid very little regard to the wonders of nature that has not often remarked this feat.

This air-to-air transference of fuel is indeed a beautiful process to watch, the parent hovering with great skill as it feeds the young on the wing. But it is characteristic of the swallow that it is a master pilot, skilled in aerobatics and aerial combat,

The Swallow's wide gape sweeps up insects like a trawl net

swerving, banking, jinking with perfect control; the bird is completely at home in its aerial territory. Apart from time spent at the nest, it is a bird of the open air, wheeling and skimming over new-mown pasture, around the grazing cattle, around the broad-leafed trees with their buzzing insect life. For the swallow is specially designed to catch insects on the wing; flies, beetles, moths and butterflies are all legitimate prey. It feeds entirely on insects, mostly catching them in the air but also picking them off the surface of a pond or lake. Its short, broad bill opens to a wide gape as it flies, scooping the unfortunate insects as if with an aerial shrimp net. At the sides of the mouth are modified contour feathers which bristle out, perhaps helping to funnel the insects into the scoop. Given the swallow's superb flying qualities and excellent sight, the insects are up against it. Watch them on a fine day, and listen to the constant clicking of the swallow's beak as it fills it with a payload of gnats.

> Swift through the air her rounds the swallow takes,
> Or sportive skims the level of the lakes.
>
> (Thomas Brown, *Pastorals*)

The swallow will drink in flight, too, taking a quick sip, and will bathe in flight, splashing into the water as it flashes by. At low levels it is adept at jinking and manoeuvring to evade obstacles, with rapid changes of course, altitude and speed. If the feeding is irresistible, it will occasionally land, but with its shuffling gait, aided by half-open wings touching the ground, it can only stagger a few paces, so the flies must indeed be thick on the ground for this technique to be worthwhile. But it can be seen on a grassy lawn if ants are swarming and about to indulge in a marriage flight, for instance.

I have seen swallows hawking long after dark, chasing the moths attracted to the brilliant floodlights of an all-night garage. And, in company with bats, they may be seen at the same activity around the stage lamps of the Minack Theatre, on the sea cliffs at Porthcurno, Cornwall, during the summer season of plays. Swallows have even been seen purposefully chasing bats, but quite what happens if they catch up with them I don't know.

Both bats and swallow come up against a serious problem towards the end of summer. But the mammal and the bird solve it in very different ways. As the days shorten and temperatures drop, there are fewer insects about. Both bats and swallows rely entirely on insect food and face a winter where it is almost unavailable. But whereas the bat survives the lean months by hibernating, living off its fat reserves and reducing energy requirements with a slowed-down metabolism, the swallows migrate to the tropics where insects fly right through the year.

Before migration, the swallows join in mass gatherings. For a while after they have left the nest, the young birds roost in it at night, but in the early autumn they gather together to form communal roosts where enormous numbers twitter and chat before sleeping. At the edge of a lake or large pond, or alongside the higher reaches of an estuary, where the tall *Phragmites* reed grows, they flock at sunset and find an unoccupied stem to grasp for the night. The intensity of the singing is remarkable, and there's a general atmosphere of bonhomie. These gatherings are a prelude to long-distance migration, but until fairly recently the generally-held belief of science was that the birds were preparing to emulate bats and hibernate for the winter. But instead of finding caves and secret holes like bats, the swallows were said to be preparing to work their way down the reed stems into the water, and to snuggle into the soft mud under its surface, there to sleep away the winter. And while it is easy now to smile at this ignorance, it was never difficult to make a good case for the theory. Aristotle firmly believed that birds hibernated in holes in the ground, and gives it as fact that naked swallows had been found in a comatose state, waiting only for the spring sun to warm them and clothe them with a new suit of feathers. Much later, in 1555, Olans Magnus, the king of Norway, writing about swallows at their autumn reed-bed gatherings, said that 'They join bill to bill, wing to wing, and foot to foot, and after a most sweet singing fall down to pools and lakes, whence in the spring they receive a new resurrection.' As further proof of their watery hibernation, he told of fishermen bringing up torpid swallows in their nets. In 1703 'A Person of Learning' vouchsafed that in fact the swallows migrated – to the moon. And yet another belief was that to assist their passage across the oceans each swallow carried a liferaft in the shape of a little stick on which to take the occasional rest.

Late in the eighteenth century, in Gilbert White's time, naturalists were still not sure about the facts. One of the puzzling aspects of the case was that, while the great majority of the swallows had disappeared from view by mid-October, nevertheless there were frequent sightings of both house martins and swallows well into November, and even December. How could these birds possibly build up the fat reserves required for a great journey of several thousands of miles? And, indeed, it seems highly likely that the greater part of these birds from third broods, hatching so late in the year, must perish on the journey. White felt that they might live in holes in the sea cliffs, emerging in warm weather to hunt, in much the same way as bats. But nevertheless he felt sure that most swallows migrated, while only a few remained, hidden, for the winter. The truth is that a very few swallows do stay for the winter, though they certainly do not hibernate naked in muddy ponds, but face hard

Swallow, master of flight (*Eric Hosking*)

times and probable starvation. The number which overwinter successfully must be very small. Shortage of food compels the overwhelming majority to leave our shores in October.

The departure flight is fuelled by the well-stocked fat reserves the bird has built up through the insect-rich summer, and triggered by shortening days with reduced light intensity and a fall in temperature. Ringing recoveries reveal that our birds are bound for South Africa, by way of the West African coast. And one of the really spectacular sights in birdwatching is to see the sky darken at dusk with the arrival of roosting swallows dropping in to the reed beds of a Johannesburg city park.

Sadly, like the house martin, the swallow appears to be suffering a decline in numbers. Changing veterinary standards in agriculture mean there are fewer flies around farmyards and stables, and there are fewer tatty farm buildings with welcoming joists and ledges and ill-fitting doors allowing easy entrance. Doubtless the flies are preparing to fight back with a will to survive. It's difficult not to hope that some of them win through, because there'd be no summer without swallows.

9 PIGEON . . . BEEF ON THE WING

There are several pigeons which are everyday birds to many of us. The wood pigeon, with its white wing-band and white neck-patch, much shot at in the country but tame and welcomed in gardens and cities; the dusky-brown collared dove with its narrow black half-collar, a recent arrival to these islands but common and completely at home in towns and villages, often nesting in a clump of conifers; even the stock dove, smaller than the wood pigeon and lacking the white markings, which used to be fairly common in the parks of central London and is still seen there. But the best candidate for everyday bird is the street pigeon, or feral pigeon, a bird with an ancient lineage and long history of relationship with man. The birds we see strutting about in city squares, begging for scraps, flying off to roost on buildings and nest in ventilator holes and in secret places behind

Homing Pigeons

The 15th century Dovecot at Old Basing House, as it was in 1899.

public statues, can claim direct descendance from the wild rock
pigeons of the sea coast of thousands of years ago.

'Pigeon' and 'dove' are interchangeable words to the
ornithologist, and it is not easy to draw a line between them.
All belong to the order Columbidae. But, in non-scientific
terms, the smaller species are doves, the larger pigeons. And
when poets are looking for an image of gentle innocence, purity
and virtue, they usually turn to the dove, with the added bonus
that it rhymes with love. Whatever you call it, the bird is
greatly used as a symbol of fertility, not surprisingly since
though it only lays two eggs to a clutch it may successfully breed
nine or ten clutches in a year, an astonishing performance – and
a characteristic that has been well and truly taken advantage of
by man.

It seems likely that the pigeon was the first bird to be
domesticated, thus having its daily regime and breeding
programme controlled by man. With its remarkable breeding
cycle and undemanding food requirements, along with an easily
satisfied specification for nesting sites, it was always a prime
candidate for domestication. In addition, it had an easy-going
disposition and tolerance of man.

The wild rock pigeon breeds naturally on ledges in coastal
caves and forages for seeds along the coast. Probably the first of
these birds to be domesticated were in the eastern Mediterranean. There are images of the pigeon in art dating back to
3100 BC, and certainly the birds were used as a source of food in
Egypt before 2600 BC. In early cultures they were sacred birds,
associated with Astarte, the goddess of love and fertility. In
India, as birds sacred to the Hindu religion, they colonised
buildings and temples without hindrance and without being
exploited for food. In classical Greece they were associated with
Aphrodite, as love-symbols. The Romans linked pigeons with
Venus in the same way, but prudently took advantage of their
culinary qualities and also used them as messengers. 'Many
persons have quite a mania for pigeons – building towers for
them on the top of their roofs, and taking pleasure in relating

the pedigree and noble origin of each,' said Pliny the Elder (AD 23–79) in his *Natural History*.

The Romans were enthusiastic pigeon-fanciers and they must have built pigeon cities, or columbaria, in England. Whether the Saxons did so is not clear, but the word 'cote' refers in part to a bird house, and 'culver', though less widespread, probably refers to the wood pigeon and gives rise to 'culver house'. 'Doo-cot' is clear enough, and indeed the Scots have indulged in pigeon culture for a very long time. Near the village of Wemyss, in Fife, there is a beach cave with dozens of man-made ledges cut out of its walls, clearly designed to encourage rock pigeons. On the wild Gower coast of Wales a cliff fissure has been built up to form a hollow pigeon buttress, with stairway access for the pigeon keeper and cliff entrance for the birds. These were both devices for tempting the wild rock pigeons to nest, so that man could take a proportion of the squabs.

The intensive rearing of domesticated birds for fresh meat, especially in winter, really began with the Norman invasion, when the conquerers brought the science of the 'colombier' with them. No twelfth-century castle was complete without its rows of pigeon holes, carefully built into a turret or high place, sheltered and southfacing. And soon the gentle pigeon became associated with less warlike places, the substantial stone-built dovecote being an important part of any manor house or monastery.

By the late thirteenth century, a medieval bishop on his travels would expect a high standard of victualling, with a table liberally provided with birds and poultry. On tour, his chaplain would record disbursements for wine, beer, beef and so on. One such record tells us of His Lordship's purchase of '2 carcasses of beef 9/4, 25 geese 5/2½, 24 pigeons 8d'. At the particular place where they were staying he records that there 'was a mill, a dove cote, a fishery, a flood gate, a passage over the wye'. And on Sundays and Holy Days, they would have a dozen pigeons as a treat. So, along with the fish pond and the rabbit warren and the duck decoy, the dove cote was an important piece of

Pigeon . . . Beef on the Wing

medieval architecture. ' . . . it behoveth especially to have care
for breeding of pigeons, as well for the great commoditie they
yeelde to the kitchin, as for the profit and yearely revenue that
they yeelde (if there be good store of corne seeldes) in the
Market' (Conradus Heresbachius, *Husbandrie*).

The pigeon house was always carefully sited, to provide
protection from prevailing winds. The Norman design involved
a circular building, solidly planted on the ground with walls
three feet thick, no windows, gradually tapering, at the very
top of the roof, to a 'lantern', which gave entrance for the birds.
A single door at ground level allowed entrance for the pigeon
keeper. Inside, the walls were covered with row after row of
pigeon-holes, 'three handfulles in length, and ledged from hole
to hole for them to walke upon'. An ingenious device called a
'potence' allowed the keeper to reach any nest by means of a
ladder which rotated on a central pillar passing within a couple
of inches of the wall as it was pushed around. The interior was
dim, to the liking of the pigeons, and each pair of birds had a
double nest site, because before one set of squabs is ready to
leave the nest the hen might well have laid her next clutch of
eggs.

As time went by the pigeon houses improved in design, and
especially in areas lacking local stone they would be built of
timber or brick, and set on pillars – which had the great benefit
of giving protection from predators such as rats, cats, weasels
and squirrels. Hawks and owls were also a problem, and the
entrance holes were carefully planned to exclude unwanted
visitors. But what suits a pigeon is also attractive to other
species. 'I found of late in myne own Dovehouse, an Owle
sitting solemnly in the Nest upon her Egges in the middest of all
the Pigions. Though the Owle seem to be greater than the
Pigion, by reason of the thickness of hir feathers, yet will creep
in at as little a place as the Pigion will: so small and little is their
bodies, though they be bombased with feathers' (Heresbachius,
1577).

Up on the roof, the pigeons would have a promenading area,

101

sheltered from cold winds and facing south to catch the best of the sun. Under the whole structure there might well be room for a stable or cow house, giving the additional benefit of extra warmth in winter, to encourage breeding. Everything was done to aid these 'wondrous fruitefull' birds. Each year the best of the early squabs were carefully selected for future breeding. The less satisfactory – 'unfruitful and naughtie coloured, and otherwise faulty' – quickly found themselves fattened and on their way to the kitchen. But the right to husband pigeons was a privilege enjoyed only by the chosen few – the nobility, the Lord of the Manor and the clergy. No one else was in the club.

In any case, unless you could lay your hands on spare corn in the dark days of winter, it was impossible to feed the birds through the difficult months. But they could be a very worthwhile proposition.

In the seventeenth century, writing of the great and far-flung estates of the Berkeley family of Gloucestershire, John Smyth recorded: 'In each manor, and almost upon each farm house he had a pigeon house, and in divers manors two. And in Hame and a few other (where his dwelling houses were) three: from each house he drew yearly great numbers. As 1300, 1200, 1000, 850, 700, 650 from an house. And from Hame one year 2151 young pigeons.' These squabs must have represented an important source of revenue, fetching 2d a dozen, a great sum of money at that time.

Not only the fat squabs had value: for the plentiful droppings which piled conveniently on the dovecote floor were rich in nitrogen and minerals. 'Doves dung is best of all others for Plants and Seeds, and may be scattered when anything is sown together with the seed, or any time afterwards. One basketful thereof is worth a cartload of Sheeps dung. Our countrymen also are wont to sow Doves dung together with their grain' (Francis Willughby, *The Ornithology*, 1678). In Persia the dung was used to fertilise the melon fields, and in south-west France, where it was used in the vineyards, dovecotes were often kept as much for the value of the dung as the squabs.

Dung was also used in the tannery process, in removing hair from the hides, and as part of the process of making saltpetre for gunpowder; also as a specific against the plague and the palsie. 'The flesh of young pigeons is restorative and useful to recruit the strength of such as are getting up or newly recovered from some great sickness' (Willughby).

One way and another, both the Lord of the Manor and the Church regarded their exclusive rights as of great value, and it was many years before the social abuses of the system were righted. The problem was simply stated. Pigeons might well be housed by and belong to one man, but they flew free and ranged widely, taking their corn wherever they could find it. In the early seventeenth century the jurist John Selden could write:

> Some men may make it a case of conscience, whether a man may have a pigeon house, because his pigeons eat other folks' corn. But there is no such thing as conscience in the business: the matter is, whether he be a man of such quality that the state allows him to have a dove house: if so, there is an end of the business: his pigeons have a right to eat where they please themselves.

But it is only too easy to imagine the thoughts of the tenant-farmer or the yeoman whose corn was being eaten. And in spite of what Selden thought, pigeon law rested on shaky foundations which were not easy to sustain in the courts. So as the years went by, small farmers and freeholders built their own pigeon houses, with rows of nest holes along the walls of their barns and farmhouses. This was not without a good deal of trouble on the way; the depredations of the lordly pigeons were one of the contributory causes, for instance, of the French Revolution. New agricultural practices, making it possible to feed cattle and sheep through the winter, using root crops, have made fresh butcher's meat available throughout the year, and most pigeon houses now lie derelict.

The descendants of those wild rock pigeons have lasted well, for though they may not flourish in dovecotes they are plentiful in our streets today. But how have their wild cousins fared? Sadly, they are rare, and increasingly rarer. However, a number of small populations of the pure-bred birds exist, confined to the north and west coasts and Scottish and Irish islands: bluish-grey birds, with two striking black bars across the folded wing, neck and breast an iridescent purple and green. The species is in decline partly because of the use of toxic seed-dressings, and perhaps because it was in direct competition with the stock dove; the catastrophic use of toxic agrichemicals in the late fifties knocked that species badly, too, but unlike the rock pigeon it has recovered. Apart from those far-flung celtic outposts of pure-bred birds, rock pigeons are now represented only by the cliffside colonies of racing pigeons which have given up the sport, and by the ubiquitous street pigeon, which itself represents a hopeless mix of long-ago-escaped dovecote stock and more recent racing-pigeon drop-outs. Mixed or not, all domestic pigeons, racers, dovecot, messenger and fancy breeds owe common ancestry to the rock pigeon.

Feral street pigeons choose nest sites which owe a lot to those ancestral sea-caves: ledges under railway bridges, ventilation holes, roof overhangs, crevices behind statues, ornamental window railings, etc – with the tidal roar of traffic flowing below. Foraging over the open spaces of the streets and parks, they prefer grain when they can get it, grass and weed seeds as second-best. But mostly they rely on handouts of bread and scraps. Fortunate for them that many people in towns are lonely, and feeding birds is one of the ways in which they can establish a relationship with a fellow creature. The population of pigeons in towns and cities would reduce itself very sharply if people stopped feeding them, but in spite of official encouragement that event is highly unlikely.

As a seed-eater programmed to swallow its food whole, the feral pigeon is sometimes seen in trouble with man-sized sandwiches. A quick flick of the head will dislodge a swallowable piece, often enough, provided the bread is reasonably soft. But in cold winter months it's useless offering large lumps of frozen old bread to pigeons: they are quite unable to deal with it. What's more, a few crumbs of cheese will do them a lot more good! Crusts of bread are of course quite foreign to the birds' natural diet, seeds and berries. But once they've learnt the drill they soon recognise the particular behaviour of a person distributing largesse; and then they will learn to identify the generous individual from the rest of the crowd, if he has a regular delivery pattern.

Birds have a two-stage stomach system. When the food has been treated with digestive enzymes in number one, the number two section – the gizzard – has the grinding job of milling the grain. The gizzard is lined with ridges and strong muscles, which work in conjunction with some deliberately swallowed small stones. The effect is mill-like, and the hardest food, like corn seeds or bread crust, can be crushed. In a sense, this is the nearest thing to teeth a bird achieves.

As for drinking, the pigeon will go to drink from a rain-water puddle, but much prefers a sweeter source if it's available. And his technique differs from that of most other species. There are of course many different drinking methods amongst birds. Swallows will take a quick sip from the surface of a pond as they fly by; tree-living species may sip from leaves after rain; blackbirds will fill the bill with water then raise the head to let the liquid run down the throat. But pigeons imbibe continuously – they suck the water up – without raising their heads. This was noticed a couple of thousand years ago by Pliny: 'It is a peculiarity of the pigeon and the turtle dove not to throw back the neck when drinking, but to take the water at a long draught, just as beasts of burden do.'

One of the pleasures of pigeon-watching is to see their mastery of flight. The wings are designed for continuous fast flapping, giving high endurance and the ability to forage over great distances. They have the power of near-vertical take off,

(*Overleaf*) Pigeons, ducks, geese and gulls in a London park (*S.C.Porter*)

wonderful manoeuvrability which allows them to dodge trees, buses and people with ease. They have large wrist-slots which allow for a low stalling speed, giving plenty of control in difficult landing situations. As a pigeon makes its final approach it extends the forewing flaps – the spurs of feathers attached to the thumb on each wing – to maintain this slow speed control. This keeps the wing working as long as possible by increasing the area. Using aids like this it can make a highly-controlled approach and a perfect touchdown.

In display, the cock bird shows off its slow wing-beat technique, and glides over the courting arena with stiffly raised wings. On the ground it stretches high, bows and circles the hen, nodding and cooing with puffed-out throat, tail spread and dusting the ground. The nest is a perfunctory affair of a few twigs or bits of straw, and pigeons are not averse to using such man-provided materials as wire, paperclips and hairpins. And the two smooth white eggs may be laid at any time through the year, though there is a breathing space during the autumn moult.

> On some few bits of sticks two white eggs lie,
> As left by accident all lorn and bare,
> Almost without a nest; yet by and by
> Two birds in golden down will leave the shells
> And hiss and snap at wind-blown leaves that shake
> Around their home where green seclusion dwells.
>
> (John Clare, *Doves*)

The incubation period is seventeen days, and the young are fed at first with 'pigeon's milk', one of the dispensations which allow pigeons so much latitude in breeding season, for the nestlings are not dependent on a particular food being available for their critical first days. But for all that the nursing parents must feed well at this time, and if they can get them they will eat the caterpillars and snails which in the ordinary way they avoid. The formation of the milk is controlled by a hormone – prolactin – and it is produced by both hen and cock in the last days of incubation in order to ensure protein supplies to the newly-hatched chick for the first few days of its life. The milk is secreted from the lining of the parent's crop. When the chick is hatched, the parent takes the squab's bill into its mouth, the squab automatically reaches in deeper, and the parent regurgitates the crop milk. After a few days, the milk is supplemented with choice pieces of soft food or seeds. And as time goes by the ratio changes so that the young are getting less and less milk, the change being controlled by hormone secretion.

In five weeks or so the squabs leave the nest, when the parents may already have been sitting on the next clutch of eggs for some time. No wonder they have always been symbols of fertility.

Otherwise, their success is, on the face of it, something of a puzzle. They carry no weapons of attack or defence, no hooked bills or sharp talons. They produce a small number of helpless chicks and have feeding habits which are not particularly flexible. On top of this they are good to eat, much enjoyed by

Pigeons in Trafalgar Square (*Jane Burton*)

everything from peregrine falcon to man. The fact remains that they are plentiful, and have always been plentiful for as long as records have been kept. You will find pigeons of one sort or another everywhere in the world. Long may they flourish.

10 THE DABBLING . . . DUCK

The mallard, or wild duck, is something of a Jekyll and Hyde character. Flighting to the wild saltmarsh it is shy and cautious; wintering in city parks it soon joins with the locals and begs for bread. But wherever you find it, it makes itself known with one of the most easily recognised calls, that raucous quacking. The drake has a rather higher pitched and shorter quack, a more subdued performance altogether. As for identification, the mallard must be one of the most immediately recognised birds. The drake has a pale-grey back, glossy dark-green head, yellow bill, white collar and purplish-brown chest. The duck is dull brown by comparison but, like the drake, has the bright-blue wing patch or speculum.

Widely distributed, mallards range from Arctic tundra to Mediterranean, by way of St James's Park. High country to low

From the Mallard (left) many domestic forms are derived, including the Silver Crested and Aylesbury Ducks

Duck Decoy

Ducks on the pond will approach and mob a small dog which appears from behind the screens. It entices them into the curved pipe so the decoyman can drive them into the tunnel net at the end.

country, they are fairly easily pleased in their living requirements, though water is never very far away, whether it is lake or pond, wild estuary or town reservoir. They have well-developed mobility, with a near-vertical take-off and a strong, purposeful flight.

The truly wild birds feed mainly at night, made cautious by centuries of persecution. On fields and saltmarshes they search for grain, berries and potatoes, but they will eat almost anything, including insects, worms, snails, frog- and fish-spawn. In brackish ditches and muddy places they up-end and dabble, staying mostly on the surface though they may on occasion dive. With a specially modified bill they sieve small particles of food from soft mud or water. On the whole they prefer their food to be from the water. They'll stir up mud to release the clouds of algae and small insects. Deep water provides little by way of food but it has its use, providing the ducks with a safe roosting area, out of the way of predators.

They swim very well indeed, of course – 'to swim like a duck' is a proverbial accomplishment. Their feet are webbed and act as paddles. The legs are set well back on the body, providing the most powerful propulsion in the water; but on land the bird is at a disadvantage and tends to waddle. Most birds have their legs set just behind their centre of gravity, maintaining balance with their toes, but swimmers – water birds – have them placed well aft where they act as the vessel's screws. (This is seen at its most extreme in the divers, which have the utmost difficulty in moving on land. And penguins sometimes find it easier to toboggan than to walk. But once in the sea they are very much at home.)

Those well-developed thigh muscles serve the duck well for swimming and up-ending, but they also have attractions for the hungry hunter. And in the days before deep-freezes and intensive agriculture made us almost independent of season, the arrival of airborne meat flying in at the onset of hard weather must have seemed a miraculous convenience. Whereas pigeons provided winter meat in return for a certain amount of husbandry and year-round co-habitation, the wild duck just arrived out of the blue, table-ready. And through the years they have successfully endured all forms of trap, ambush, decoy, punt-gun and shot gun, and still visit us in numbers every winter — living proof of the conservation truism that the relationship between predator and prey is beneficial to both species. The wary mallard has always been regarded as a worthy quarry in the exacting sport of wildfowling.

Of all the trapping methods the most successful has been the pipe-decoy. Dating back to the sixteenth century, at one time there were as many as two hundred in operation in Britain. Even today several are still in use, in the service of bird-ringing for scientific purposes. At the New Grounds, in Gloucestershire, Peter Scott's Wildfowl Trust has a fine example, and there is another at Abbotsbury, in Dorset, operated by the swanherd, Fred Lexter. At Orielton, in Pembrokeshire, the Field Studies Council now have the remains of a once-active decoy. I have spent many happy hours patching up the netting, in order to trap and ring a few wigeon or teal or mallard. But in the old days the birds were trapped for the kitchen.

The decoy involved a lake or pond, sometimes man-made, surrounded by quiet, undisturbed woodland. From the open water radiated several ditches, leading into the vegetation. The ditches were enclosed with funnel-nets, stretched over hoops, and these pipes tapered as the ditch curved to a dead end with a purse net. Tame decoy ducks dabbled inside the pipe, feeding on corn, attracting the wild ones to join them. Reed screens prevented the ducks from seeing the decoyman and his dog, a vital assistant to the procedure. For when the trained dog showed himself at the entrance to the pipe the nearest ducks would react in a manner typical of the species: they would 'mob' him in much the same way that small birds will chase an owl. Now the trained dog showed himself in carefully planned gaps in the reed screen, each time leading the ducks deeper into the pipe. At the critical moment the man showed himself at the pipe entrance and the ducks flew away from him, towards the dead end of the funnel, thus ending in the purse net. The 'Judas' ducks quietly swim back into the pipe, unafraid of the approaching man. One of the beauties of the system was that the whole operation could be carried out without disturbing the main flock of ducks which remained on the open pond; the decoyman could make several catches from the same flight of duck. In one season 31,200 ducks, including teal and wigeon, were sent to London from ten decoys in Lincolnshire. The trade was licensed by Act of Parliament, the season lasting from late October through to February.

Not all roast duck flew in from the Arctic, of course. The domestic version pre-dates the gun and decoy-pipe by many hundreds of years. All domesticated ducks are descended from the wild mallard, possibly first tamed in Asia a very long time ago. Certainly by Roman times they were an important food source. The eggs were collected from wild nests, then brooded by farmyard fowls. Even today, broody bantams are used when setting a clutch of duck eggs, as they make such ideal mothers. Nowadays there are a number of varieties of domestic duck, differing greatly in shape, size and function, some used for meat and some for egg production. In the process of domestication man calls the tune and speeds up the process of evolution. By selecting specimens with desired features from which to breed he can increase the rate of genetic variation. Thus he may produce fancy shapes and colours for 'the fancy' or he may select for precocious egg-laying, or muscle bulk. Whereas the wild mallard drake weighs an average of $2\frac{1}{2}$ lb, the Aylesbury, result of a thousand years of selection, weighs about 9 lb. Wild mallards lay a clutch of about ten eggs, only once in a season, but ducks bred for egg-laying will behave like domestic fowl and lay daily through the larger part of the year.

So the mallard appears in two guises: as the wary bird of the wild saltmarsh and as the tame farmyard or city-park free-loader. There is a certain amount of overlap between the two, because the population in urban parks is much increased in winter, especially if weather further north is severe. And then the wild birds which join the residents soon become surprisingly tame. In cities, ducks tend to commute between feeding areas and roosting reservoirs and sewage farms, but they are very much less inclined to feed at night and roost by day; they become more-or-less diurnal as they become used to man and are less persecuted. They patronise dockland for grain and parks for sandwiches.

It is on the ornamental ponds of city parks that you will often see the spectacular courtship dance of mallards in the spring. Several drakes may circle the chosen duck in formal attitudes – heads down, necks back – then they submerge their bill tips, stand up in the water and stroke their bills up their breasts, all the time crooning hoarsely of their desire. More up-heading and

Duck Mallard
calling her young from their nest in a pollarded willow

tailing follows, with apparently random swimming. Then the merry-go-round starts all over again, with maybe a wild chase thrown in. If the duck is caught, she may be seized by the neck and held down with her head underwater. So rough is the courtship that, in his amorous exertions, the drake may even hold her underwater too long, so that she drowns.

Though the mallard nests on the ground in the wild, protected by a bramble bush, or in a reedy clump on an island, in urban areas it tends to get a bit of height between it and the likely predators – cats, dogs and small boys. In St James's Park, for instance, where they nest regularly, they patronise holes in elms and black poplars. In the five-acre lake they enjoy Duck Island, the site of an old pipe decoy built in 1665. But elsewhere they show a predilection for holes in pollarded willows, quiet roof gardens, or flower boxes. The nest may be as much as thirty feet off the ground. Rafts or barges may be pressed into service, the main requirement being lack of disturbance, and proximity to food and water. They will take readily to man-provided sites, duck-baskets placed on top of rafts moored away from the pond or river-bank, for instance.

The nest is built by the duck, a mound of dead leaves and grasses, lined with feathers and down. And she lays anything up to fifteen or sixteen greyish-green or greenish-buff eggs, although about ten is a normal clutch. While the drake stands guard, the duck incubates for twenty-eight days. When she leaves the nest for a short feeding period, she carefully covers the eggs, the large number being conspicuous and not particularly well camouflaged. Covering them with the soft down feathers helps to keep them warm. When the ducklings hatch, they are already covered with downy feathers of their own, and they leave the nest soon after they have dried. Now the duck must lead them to the water, a task which may take them over a few yards of grassy bank, or may mean a major expedition first down to street level and then across a busy thoroughfare. This is the moment beloved of photographers, when a policeman halts the traffic as the new mother leads her

Mallard with young (*D.N.Dalton*)

ducklings across the road and through the park railings and down to the safety of the pond, where the day-old birds take to swimming and feeding – well, like ducks to water!

The drake has surprisingly little to do in all this, but hovers about nearby. Although wild mallard only bring off one clutch, in settled and protected conditions semi-domesticated birds may achieve two. But the late summer is not the best time of the year for the drake, since he goes into 'eclipse' plumage when he moults, looking generally dark-brown and uninteresting, a camouflage ideally suited for a time when his flight feathers need replacement. In the park, he is a nondescript shadowy figure at this time of year. In the wild, with his family of growing ducklings in the Arctic wastes, he keeps a low profile, feeds as best he may, and grows a fine new coloured flying suit in preparation for the migration flight to the mild winter of Britain. There he might join the easy-riders on the village duck-pond, or he might rough it on the estuary mudflats. A two-faced bird, but both faces are attractive.

NOW BIRD ON . . .
FURTHER PLEASURE FROM BIRDWATCHING

Enjoy more birding as a member of the *Royal Society for the Protection of Birds.* Founded in 1889, its quarter of a million members represent a powerful and forward-looking association of people with a common interest in birds and nature conservation. Professional staff manage more than fifty superb reserves, enforce protection laws and initiate scientific research as well as encouraging much useful education work. Regional offices organise local meetings. *Young Ornithologists' Club* for children. Magazine, sales catalogue. Write for details to RSPB, The Lodge, Sandy, Beds, and please join!

As you become more involved in the intricacies of birding and bird behaviour, you may wish to take an active part in bird research. Join the *British Trust for Ornithology*, Beech Grove, Tring, Herts. The BTO issues newsletters and a quarterly journal, and co-ordinates research activities such as ringing and census work.

Wildlife (243 King's Road, London SW3 5EA) is a general natural-history magazine, issued monthly, which includes much of interest to birdwatchers. But the birders' special pride and joy is the monthly journal *British Birds* (Macmillan Journals Ltd, 4 Little Essex St, London WC2R 3LF). This is indispensable for all serious ornithologists, publishing papers, notes and excellent photographs on the birds of the western palearctic, and acting as a clearing house for bird information.

For a general introduction to birdwatching, read James Fisher and Jim Flegg's book *Watching Birds*, published by T. & A.D.

Poyser, 1975. Two other of James Fisher's books also make civilised reading: *The Shell Bird Book*, published by Michael Joseph in 1966, and *The World of Birds*, which he wrote with Roger Tory Peterson in 1964 (Macdonald).

Now you must get a straightforward identification book, such as *A Field Guide to the Birds of Britain and Europe*, by Peterson, Mountfort and Hollom. Get the most recent edition, published by Collins (and get the prospectus for Collins' magnificent series 'The New Naturalist' at the same time). And to strengthen your bird library with some meat and backbone, providing basic information about the lifestyle of all the British species, get hold of *The Popular Handbook of British Birds*, by P.A.D. Hollom (published by Witherby). This valuable and up-dated distillation from the aged five-volume *Handbook of British Birds* serves us well until the long-promised *Birds of the Western Palearctic* sees the light of day. Use it in conjunction with a bound set of *British Birds*, and you will be well served with information.

Birdtables and nestboxes provide an enormous amount of innocent pleasure, and *The New Bird Table Book*, by Tony Soper (published by David & Charles) may help to increase and inform that pleasure.

For general enjoyment try some of these:

The Charm of Birds, by Edward Grey
The Natural History of Selborne, by Gilbert White
Letters from Skokholm, by R.M. Lockley
Shearwaters, by R.M. Lockley
Adventure Lit their Star, by Kenneth Allsopp
The Life of the Robin, by David Lack
A Study of Blackbirds, by D.W. Snow
Birds of Town and Country, by Eric Simms

The main tools of birdwatching, apart from an enquiring mind, are fieldglasses, notebook and pen. Charles Frank Ltd, 144 Ingram Street, Glasgow G1, have a very useful free booklet 'Tell me, Mr. Frank' which introduces you to the complexities of binoculars, and they offer a good range for sale. There really is no need to buy the very expensive glasses, superb though they are; for everyday practical birdwatching, the Japanese version is virtually indistinguishable and a good deal cheaper. Having got that unhappy truth off my chest, and having no axe to grind, I recommend the Swift range, but it is impossible to suggest the 'best' size of magnification etc, for birdwatching. It depends where and when and how you do your birding. I almost always use 7x50, because I spend most time afloat, and that is the best marine size. If you watch from the comfort and stability of your sitting-room, then you might enjoy a high magnification, provided you use a tripod or fixing of some kind. 8x30 or 9x35 glasses make useful general-purpose tools. But read the booklet, and see the advertisements in the RSPB magazine *Birds*.

Photography is a pleasant hobby and may on occasion be a useful adjunct to scientific birding. Some useful books are Eric Hosking and John Gooders' *Wildlife Photography*, 1975; J. Warham's *The Technique of Photographing Birds*, 1956; Russ Kinne's *The Complete Book of Nature Photography*, 1962. For movie photography, more expensive than still work, amazing though that may seem to anyone who is hooked on cameras try Christopher Parsons' *Making Wildlife Movies*, 1971. Doubtless all the books I've suggested may be borrowed from the local library.

INDEX

Index